Grandma Gjertrud's

BEDTIME STORIES
Nurturing the Child Within

GUNNHILD WIK MIKKELSEN

Grandma Gjertrud's Bedtime Stories
Nurturing the Child Within

Copyright © 2015 Gunnhild Wik Mikkelsen

Published by:
Transformation Books
211 Pauline Drive #513
York, PA 17402
www.TransformationBooks.com

ISBN: 978-0-9862901-7-6
Library of Congress Control No: 2015948668

Cover design by: Kristin Granli, *www.KristinGranli.no*
Layout and typesetting by: Ranilo Cabo
Editor: Marlene Oulton, *www.MarleneOulton.com*
Proofreader: Allison Saia
Back Cover Photo: Signe Hultgren

Printed in the United States of America

Grandma Gjertrud's
BEDTIME STORIES
Nurturing the Child Within

Dedication

To my grandmother, Kari Wik and all the other grandmothers in the world who strive to make a difference to their loved ones.

Acknowledgements

Many people are to be thanked for their contribution to my being able to write this book. Naming them all would be impossible, but I will do my best to try to give you an impression of the diversity of contributors to its content.

First, my great grandmother Andrea Wik is to be thanked. By offering to adopt a child that was not wanted, thereby giving him the possibility of a life and later becoming my mother's father. My Grandmother Kari Wik was the first to introduce me to the secret life of plants and their healing powers, while the naturopathic doctor of our family, Dr. Backe Reinertsen, opened my eyes to the world of seeing and healing, making sure my diseased years of childhood did not become a chronic condition.

All my grandparents – Kari, Kristian, Ebba and Gunelius, for teaching me to enjoy gardening, farming, handicrafts, old traditions, and music as well as all the unmarried ancestors of my family that loved me as a child and presented my home with wonderful, fascinating and exciting subjects from all around the world through inheritance.

My mother, Ragnhild Karoline, who taught me by her own example, to trust my intuition. My sister, Kjellaug, who with her true thoroughness and willingness, helped me translate to English some of the stories that were already written in Norwegian. My brother, Terje, for providing me with writing accompaniment from the most wonderful interpretations of classical composers through his many CD productions as a conductor. My father, Karl Henrik, who has driven me and all my gear in his car, later with an additional trailer behind containing my homemade herbal teas and decocts, dog, goats and many belongings, to the most rural and strange places, always with patience and great packing skills – you're the best!

My foster son, Anders, for gifting me with the wonderful experience of being a mother.

ACKNOWLEDGEMENTS

To Jon Godal and his crew at Fosen Folkehøgskole, for creating an arena for honoring the wisdom to be found in old traditions and knowledge. To Bent Andersen, an excellent blacksmith that I could watch for hours, a well-read, highly interesting conversation partner on nightly sailing trips along the Norwegian coast, and my eye-opener to the unknown. I miss your humorous comments!

To Hans Øen, a typical small scale farmer, faithful, thorough, hard-working man, honoring his ancestors by caring for all that they created, and yet waiting all his life for the wife that he wanted to come find him. Thank you for letting me into your wonderful life, as well as sharing your farm and wisdom.

To the 120 inhabitants of the little island Selvær in northern Norway who included me and my friends in their community and generously shared with us their knowledge on how to survive and live together, support each other, keep together and share their daily life and struggles despite huge differences in religion and lifestyle.

To all my wonderful landladies who have rented me their precious, beautiful, sometimes small, old houses for an affordable price to my tight budget; Gjertrud Hornemann, Magnhild Myklebust, Klara Bruland, Eva and Edvin Thorson, Helle Margrethe Meltzer, Cecilie Meltzer and Gunvor Wittersø.

To my dear dog, Bille, who kept guard by my side, followed me in the years of least money and most travel with his great capability of disappearing underneath the seat or behind my skirt (although being a rather large Berner Sennen dog), making sure he would never stop me from getting the much desired hitchhike ride with a long distance truck, nor give me the additional cost of having to pay for a dog.

To my two professors, Norun Askeland and Bente Aamotsbakken, founders of Norway's first BA, later Master's degree study in non-fiction, from whom I learned to bring non-fiction into fiction through storytelling. And to Ingvild Handagard who taught me how to plan a book the American way, using filing cards (instead of the Norwegian way of writing and rewriting, and then cutting and gluing the text together) which worked wonders for the layout of this book. And to the participants of Grotids seminars, where non-fiction writer's come together during a weekend a year and discuss their writing.

ACKNOWLEDGEMENTS

To Francis Treuhertz for introducing me to the world of classical homeopathy and other important skills of life. To Paul Herscu and Amy Rothenberg for teaching me how to observe and describe what I see. To Leo for his commitment and willingness to contribute to our possibility of understanding. And to all my clients and patients who have taught me more about life by sharing their life stories with me – thank you.

To Judith Berky for her early feedback on the feminine topics of this book. To Ragnhild Sekne for her willingness to always give her feedback on my questions however late at night I contacted her. To Grethe Lous for bringing me into new, interesting settings, and for her weekly energy forecasts that I have come to appreciate. To Kirsten Stendevad at the Goddess school in Denmark for introducing the Goddess toolbag in a new wrapping. To Tove Marie Dimmock for being the one person in my life making sure to call me every day, lifting up my life over and over again, and always having a comment to spare on my progress in writing as in life. To Tone Krohn for always seeing the best in me and recognizing my capabilities. To Pamela Pieters for working with me week after week to improve the language and dialogs – you have taught me a lot. To Soleira Green, my great inspiration and wonderful co-traveler in space.

To my great Hero through lifetimes, for admiring my brains and loving my persona, and for lending me your favorite CD.

To Brendon Burchard for his excellent training and for the magnificent Experts Academy in September 2011 that introduced me to communities on Facebook who later, invited me to join the worldwide "It's Your Life" summit as one of nine speakers. Thank you, Lauchlan Mackinnon, for introducing me! That is also where I got to know Susan M. Davis who, out of the blue, offered to help me get my book written. Thank you, for believing in me at this stage, and for the enormous load of work you did helping me produce my entire manuscript for a competition in 2012. I really look forward to finally meeting you in person, Susan, at my launch party! Thanks also to Vivian Napp for keeping up with our weekly Skype talks.

To Olsen Nauen Bell Foundry, close to my home, that since 1844 has produced the most wonderful bells – big or small, church bells and space clearing bells. Thank you for opening my eyes to the wonderful world of magical bell sounds.

To Kristin Granli, my one and only illustrator, that also this time managed to condense all my wishes for

ACKNOWLEDGEMENTS

the book cover and still add her professional qualities, making sure the final product would fit the legacy of the book.

To Mary Hark in Australia, for her willingness to explore the exercises in the book and give me feedback. And to Lena Gjertine Bakken for being the first person to not only use the exercises in the book on herself and her inner child, but even on her real life children, assuring me that the exercises worked very well also in helping them.

If you think that a woman can run her farm all by herself, write a book, and live a life, well, think again. Great honors go to the backup team that helps me care for my properties and animals whilst I am away. Jackson the Greatest, Signe Hultgren, Randi Beck, Elfi Sverdrup, Øivind Horntvedt, Ketil Rivaa, Britt Andersen, Ole Christian Torkildsen, Even Homb, Grethe and Odd, Per Richard, and my tenants upstairs. Without you I would be lost – simple as that.

And finally, a thank you to my publisher, Transformation Books. To Tami Blodgett for her quick mind and supportive teleseminars, to Carrie Jareed for keeping track of all the practical things, and to Christine Kloser who follows her heart and runs her company with the finest balance of spiritual intuition and nose for business, inspiring and making it possible for me and many others to make a difference in the world as a writer. My last thank you goes to Marlene Oulton, my editor, for making it safe for me to get those last pages written while still remaining sensitive to my own voice. I find that she adds to my text in a beautiful way.

Thank you one and all!

Introduction

Grandma Gjertrud's Bedtime Stories is a magical book. I know that description sounds a bit odd, but the more I tried to work on it, the clearer it became that this manuscript has been working on me and not the other way around.

I promise that I will explore this statement a bit further on, but let me first share with you some of the reasons why I felt compelled to write this book in the first place, as well as what I hope you'll gain from reading it.

As I was putting these words onto my computer screen, it became clear that, more or less, all of my life I have been preparing to be able to write this book. It has been a journey filled with exciting experiences. I guess I should add that as a child I had a huge interest for digging up stories. I loved to listen to older people tell tales about their lives, or those of their ancestors. As soon as I learned to read, (or so I have been told), I used to bore my friends by way too often burying my nose in a book instead of coming out to play. And I was even happier if allowed to tell entertaining stories myself to other people.

I would tell stories at the dinner table, at kindergarten, and later at school where for years I loved to bend the rules every time I had to write an assessment. Thankfully I'd get away with it as the story itself was entertaining enough to cover for the missing elements of following the teacher's instructions. Later on, when entertaining stories were not appreciated at school, I would tell them at campfires, as a babysitter, on a long ride, be it by train, bus, or car. (Fortunately my native country is large enough for long journey's which are perfect for creating travelling stories.) In my annual Christmas letters I sent back in the days before the computer made paper letters disappear, I'd regal the recipient with a condensed version of what had gone on in my life in the past year.

I also had (and still do) have a great appetite for knowledge. I wanted to know how things are made, how they work or operate, and how to fix them if needed. I could watch people do their handicrafts for hours, and the great admiration I have always had for the wisdom of elderly people started to develop back in those days.

Today I strongly believe that all the knowledge, experience, wisdom, patience, forgiveness, love, humor, and openness that elderly people contribute to our society is heavily underrated and underappreciated. So when I started planning to write a storytelling book, I knew right away that I had to include an elderly person in the storyline. And very soon that person manifested herself as Grandma Gjertrud; a name it later became clear to me was no mistake, as when you pronounce the name it sounds like the Norwegian word for "heart" – *hjerte.* In essence, Grandma Gjertrud, based upon my own lineage of great women in my life over the span of four generations, lives in my heart. My favorite teacher was my grandmother – my maternal one. We had a lot of interests in common as we both loved to collect wild plants and herbs, and we used to study my great-grandmothers old books in gothic print on how to use the different plants for medicine. But my grandmother also had other great traits to teach me. She knew how to be a "woman," and again I understand that this sounds weird, but as I grew up in the great time of femininity and equality, being a woman was actually not something I was trained to think of as something great or special, much less unique. I was brought up to think of being a woman as being allowed to compete with a man.

Not so with my grandmother. She was powerful in a soft way. She always supported her husband and made sure he was able to express himself in his uttermost and best way. She made sure her family was fed nutritious and healthy food, seeing to it that they all had their individual needs met. She also managed the farm on a very low budget and yet still found time and even some money for pleasure, music, play, laughter and just being together as a happy family. In her own manner she would still make sure she was always treated with respect.

It is her values that I hope to instill through Grandma Gjertrud's words of wisdom throughout this book. I want to inspire women everywhere to go to sleep at night knowing they have given their best to the world at large that day, and let today's bedtime story nurture their tomorrows.

But being wise and full of knowledge means nothing unless you have someone to pass on your knowledge to. In this book, thirty-six year old Karoline represents the many women who struggle in their lives, be it in their work, with their health, or in their relationships, and to make things worse, Karoline is struggling on all three levels as the book begins, so much so that she is not at all sure she is in for this game called life for very much longer. And that is when Grandma Gjertrud comes to visit.

With this book I want to inspire women to choose love over fear, and to help them find better ways of communicating and being together with their loved ones, as well as sharing their gifts with the world through their work. Storytelling is an age-old transformative method to take people beyond their daily struggles to the place where they can recreate and redesign their lives. Instead of fulfilling someone else's dream, I, just as Grandma Gjertrud does, help them reconnect with their true self and rediscover their own lost desire for life.

So far this introduction is quite ordinary. It is now that the magic starts to reveal itself.

I have told you already that I have been planning and writing this book for a long time, decades to be more specific. But three years ago, it finally started to take its shape, as it was my contribution to a writer's contest where the whole manuscript had to be delivered. I collected all my boxes of notes and suggestions, and a friend of mine whom I have never met in person, offered to proofread the chapters as soon as they were written. Luckily she was in California, nine hours behind me, while I was I Norway, meaning I could work all day, mail her a chapter or two in the evening, and wake up next morning with my chapter read, edited, and commented on freshly in my inbox! Since then only minor changes and improvements have been added, with the help of several amazing people that I have just "happened" to meet.

In the fall of 2014, I went to Baltimore to join a conference with Christine Kloser. I was ill at the time, having been bullied and criticized in my job as a foster mum. During the event, she decided to start to offer publishing possibilities for her students and clients. Since I really enjoyed and appreciated her excellent way of marrying femininity, intuition and business, I asked to join in with this book. When the time came to have an editor's response, I was surprised to hear the editor's comment, "Gunnhild, this book is really about you."

As I started to prove her wrong, I soon realized (by the amount of tears running down my cheeks as I spoke to her), that I had been writing the story of my life, even parts of my life that had not yet happened, when I began the book three years prior. I have been both touched and inspired myself when reading it over again several times these last six months. I've even been struck by the fact that some of the parts I could not even remember having written as I read them a new, clearer way. These were the parts that were most soothing to me in my new situation.

Most surprised I discovered that the character of Grandma Gjertrud had been inspired around the memory of my mother (who has been dead for quite some years), and that Karoline, who even had my mother's middle name without me having recognized that at the time, was in fact the daughter that I had never had. That the special relationship between the two of them was indeed not only my tribute to my beloved grandmother, but my way of creating a new grandmother-granddaughter relationship in my family, by giving my mother her one and only grandchild in absentia.

And to end this story of seemingly happy families, let me just add that I do not have biological children, Grandma Gjertrud did not have biological children, and my great grandmother did not have biological children. But nevertheless, we can all contribute to the new generations with all the amazing wisdom that we have to pass on.

Love comes from the heart, and as long as your heart is beating, you´re in business. ♥

Blessings,

Gunnhild Wik Mikkelsen

Table of Contents

Grandma Gjertrud Comes to Visit

Karoline's Life at Thirty-Six

"Help!" Karoline said into the darkness of her bedroom that evening. It was meant to be a shout out of clear expression of how she was feeling, but on its way out of her mouth the word lost its power and came out as a whisper.

"Help! Anyone?" she tried again. This time it sounded a bit more convincing although she was the only one to notice.

She felt like a total failure… because she was a failure. No doubt about it!

Her boyfriend was dissatisfied with her, too. He had mentioned they should consider breaking up while he was walking out the front door to go abroad on a four week lecture tour that same morning. It had taken her some hours to respond to the shock, but now, laying in their king size bed, the truth had entered her heart like a claw made from iron. She felt like a little girl that nobody wanted, and she did not like to picture herself in that role.

She would much rather see herself as the problem solver: The woman that could take any ill-tempered, misunderstood kid in any classroom and turn them into a dedicated pupil. Her great skill in understanding and communicating with children was widely known and appreciated, especially among the receivers of her efforts and their parents. The same was not to be said of her colleagues who often felt threatened by her success. Having worked many years as a teacher, Karoline felt confident she knew what she was doing when giving special attention to the troublemakers in her classroom, and did not let her colleague's opinions alter her style of teaching.

But lately her new boss had added to her problems by demanding she start respecting the new rules of the school which stated that all pupils were entitled to the same amount of attention and support. Her special kids would no longer receive special treatment, as it would be far too expensive for the school should this become the new standard of education. Karoline did not respond to her boss's demands at first, so then he started to get really domineering. This particular day he had approached her in the teacher's workroom, shouting at her to obey his rules or quit. Again, it took Karoline some hours to react to his actions. But now, hidden by the darkness in her room, she could feel tears gathering behind her eyelids, and a big, cold knot of fear was making its way through her abdomen. All she wanted was to hide under her covers and never have to face her boss again.

As if feeling small, scared, haunted, and vulnerable was not enough, Karoline had also reminded herself of some contents of a letter that had been waiting for her when she came home this afternoon.

"There are some abnormalities in your bloodwork that we need to take a closer look at," her doctor wrote in the letter. "We have therefore rescheduled you for a new appointment next week to run some more tests."

Karoline had never seen such a letter and immediately started to wonder what the abnormalities could be.

The fact that she had been rescheduled so quickly had made her worries grow, and by now she was sure it had to be cancer. A really nasty, malignant cancer. Parts of her were even welcoming the possibility of a quick, upcoming death as a nice way of escaping the whole misery of her life.

But the little girl inside her did not want to give up. She just wanted to be cared for and live. She desperately longed for someone to tuck her in and wish her goodnight like the grown-ups used to when she was a little girl. Karoline could feel how the little girl inside her seemed to have her own voice. It was fighting its way up her throat, wanting to make a statement that she had no way of stopping.

"Help! Anyone? I cannot manage any more of this!"

A strange movement in the dusky light over at her bedroom door caught Karoline's attention, immediately turning her whole body into a state of total alarm. She could feel her heart pounding, quick and hard, and her breath stopped for a few moments as her body gave all its attention to her ears. She squinted her eyes just a little bit, trying to get a better view, and for a moment a little miniature church bell glowing slightly over at her dresser caught her attention.

The strange light started to brighten, and Karoline was ready to close her eyes and hide under the bedcovers when suddenly her name was softly uttered.

"Karoline...? Honey...?"

As a ghostly form started moving toward her, Karoline could see that is was an old, matronly lady with silver gray hair divided into braids or *fletter*, nicely wrapped across the top of her head. Just when Karoline thought her heart would stop from fear, she recognized the vision as her dear Grandma Gjertrud who had passed away almost ten years ago.

"Oh my God," Karoline gasped, her eyes widening, not really believing what she was seeing.

"I suggest you keep Her out of this," Grandma Gjertrud replied, trying to hold back a giggle. "You see, I am sort of on a private, unauthorized mission here."

"Oh, Grandma Gjertrud! I am so glad to see you right now, even in my state of misery," Karoline sighed. "I can tell you still have your sense of humor. Is that appreciated on the other side, too?"

Grandma Gjertrud managed to sink down on Karoline's bed as they both were suddenly doubled over with laughter. It was the type of laughter that relieved the tension in Karoline's body, causing her to lower her shoulders and soothing her tired senses. Slowly the laughter turned into a deeply felt sobbing, with tears streaming down Karoline's face. Grandma Gjertrud, being deprived of a proper physical body, could not reach out to touch her dear granddaughter, but concentrated on sending her love and light to make her feel safe and protected.

"I heard you calling, honey," Grandma Gjertrud said. "What is happening?"

"I don't want to play this game anymore," Karoline stuttered, trying to control her crying. "I regret ever having said yes to this life. This misery is not what I signed up for at birth. People don't understand me, they don't like me, and they don't appreciate my efforts. And the people I am supposed to do my mission together with are not here either. Plus there are the ones who refuse to play by the rules. So I don't want to be here anymore. Please take me with you, Grandma Gjertrud. Don't try to make me stay here any longer!"

Grandma Gjertrud could feel all the emotions raging inside Karoline's body, and even understood how Karoline felt about life right now. But being able to use all of the wisdom and insight she had acquired from the other side, Karoline's predicament seemed so easy to adjust from her point of view.

"Have you never felt on top of the world in this lifetime?" Grandma Gjertrud asked.

"Yeeees...." Karoline hesitated in answering as she tried to remember. "When I was a little girl, I felt I totally owned the world, that I was loved and that everything was there for me to enjoy."

"I'm glad to hear you remember feeling that way," Grandma Gjertrud replied. "I, too, remember you as a charming, sparkling, happy little girl. But tell me, honey, when did that stop? What happened? Do you know?"

Karoline did not have to hesitate to find the answer. "I got scared."

"Please, fill me in on that," Grandma Gjertrud said with great interest.

"I was around six, I think. Daddy and my friend Anne's father had jobs that made them travel a lot. We were fantasizing about how great it would be when they came back home. All the nice gifts they would bring, how they would take us on their laps and tell us wonderful stories. Anne's father was the first to return. They had prepared a special meal for the occasion, and as I was there playing all day, I was delighted to be invited to join them for supper. We ate in the dining room. The table was decorated with a white tablecloth, flowers, and beautiful old china and silver. Everything was great until I happened to spill some food on the tablecloth. Then from out of nowhere, Anne's father exploded in anger and called me a lot of bad words. I froze in fear and did not dare to react or cry in case I would spoil the whole party any more than I already had. I felt that it was my fault the special meal did not turn out the way it was supposed to and I was really ashamed. When I came home I went straight to bed, not wanting to tell anyone about my mistake." Karoline seemed puzzled. "I don't understand why that scared me so much. I mean I have had people yell at me, both before and after that episode, but ever since I have always had this really insecure feeling every time someone gets angry with me. It's like I was grounded forever after that experience."

"Oh, honey, how could I not see that?" Grandma Gjertrud sighed.

"You remember it?" Karoline seemed surprised.

"I remember you coming home, very pale, but when I asked you what had happened, you assured me it was nothing special, that you were just very tired. I realize I should not have just taken your word for it, but looked inside myself to check it out. Can you forgive me for having been so blind, Karoline?" Grandma Gjertrud looked at her encouragingly. "Imagine if we could do it all over again with all my knowledge from the other side to guide us. I would love to retell your story as I believe that I can teach you how to find your way through your challenging experiences and stay fully vibrant and enthused about your life. I believe that when we are fully engaged in our lives we can contribute to maintaining peace in our homes. To me peace at home is essential for developing peace in the world. How else can people agree to peace in the world if they cannot even have peaceful relationships with their loved ones?"

"Do you really think that doing this would make a difference?" Karoline asked.

"Definitely!"

"Well..." Karoline was searching for the right words. "Let's do it then!"

"Okay," Grandma Gjertrud said. "Here's the deal. I will tell you bedtime stories seven evenings in a row. You will not be able to see me, but you will hear my voice. After the seven days, I will return to see how you are doing, making room for questions you might have about the stories I've told you during this time. Does this sound like something you'd like to do, honey?"

"Oh yesss!" Karoline exclaimed, feeling as if a little light was being lit inside her. A smile made its way to her face and her eyes started to sparkle again. "I so much needed you to come, Grandma Gjertrud. And I am really grateful that you did, but do I have to wait until tomorrow to get my first bedtime story?"

"We will, of course, start preparing right away," Grandma Gjertrud replied, smiling back at Karoline. "Tonight I will sing your favorite cradle song to make sure you get a deep, refreshing sleep. Nobody can work on their fears when they are totally exhausted. Then tomorrow evening you will have your first bedtime story. So stretch out nicely, roll over on your side, breathe thoroughly, and let me tuck you in, honey."

Karoline cuddled herself into a comfortable position, got her covers tightly pulled around her, and automatically started to take deep breaths as Grandma Gjertrud began to sing her sweet, rhythmical cradle song.

"Sweet dreams, honey," Grandma Gjertrud whispered into the silent darkness upon her departure, as Karoline was already sound asleep.

PART ONE

Karoline's Life at Six

Bedtime Story Number One

Grandma Gjertrud knew something was wrong the moment she opened the door to Karoline's room that evening. A lifetime of struggle and searching had made Grandma Gjertrud sensitive, observant, wise and caring, and now all her senses were telling her she'd better be prepared for what she might find.

Karoline's family didn't really know much about Grandma Gjertrud's life before they met her. Tired of living in a big city, they had been hunting for a farm in the countryside where they could move to for a long time when they happened to see Grandma Gjertrud's little note in a health food shop in town explaining how she was too old to run her own farm and was looking for new owners. She still wanted to go on living there, yet needed a family to join her in looking after the place. In other words, Grandma Gjertrud's living out her life on the property would be part of the deal. Having had no children of her own, Grandma Gjertrud figured this would be her best chance of becoming a grandmother as well.

Karoline's family, having no relatives close by, were thrilled by this idea. They worried that taking care of an old Granny might soon become a burden, but letting go of such a wonderful opportunity to buy a farm was not an option. Little did they know that Grandma Gjertrud would soon be contributing far more to their household than they ever imagined possible. Not only did she know a lot of handy tricks on how to run a small, old-fashioned farm, she also knew a lot about people. She could even heal you whenever you had hurt yourself physically, using whatever herb or plant or cupboard leftover was at hand.

Still, Grandma Gjertrud's best skills were the ones you couldn't really see. People took it for granted that her house and property were so pleasant to visit just because it always looked stunningly pretty; almost like paradise itself. The minute a visitor opened the gate and stepped into her domain, it seemed as if time stopped. They would start breathing more deeply and fully, their heart rate would slow down, and they would relax and feel at ease. Upon entering the cozy old kitchen and sitting on the comfortable couch opposite the fireplace, they would then find themselves in the middle of revealing their inner problems and frustrations even before Grandma Gjertrud's teapot was ready to be poured. Somehow Grandma Gjertrud knew exactly what questions to ask, enabling her visitors to dig deeper and look further ahead into finding a new solution and a better future. She let nobody out of her care until she was sure they would be fit for life again. It was so subtle, the way Grandma Gjertrud performed this magic, which made her guests feel fully present, vibrant, joyful, and – happy! Most people were unaware of the high level of consciousness Grandma Gjertrud used to perform her special brand of caring and healing.

Grandma Gjertrud loved her new granddaughter, six-year-old Karoline. But this one particular evening, when she came into her bedroom to kiss her goodnight, Grandma Gjertrud had a feeling something was wrong. She noticed the deep frown line on Karoline's forehead and took it from there. This wrinkle was just the confirmation she needed to know where to start.

Could it be fear that was causing it to appear? Worry? Hurt?

Grandma sat down by the little girl's bedside, touched her cheek with one hand, and went on to run her fingers through Karoline's golden curly hair. She opened up her heart, listening inward for what to say first, noticing with satisfaction how her own presence had already made Karoline's breathing slow down.

"Did you have a nice dinner at your friend's house this afternoon, Karoline?"

Watching Karoline take an extra, quick breath of air, Grandma knew where this was leading. Now all she needed was to get Karoline to talk. She started with the easy questions, the ones Karoline would not be able to resist answering, knowing that getting her to continue talking would be easier once she was into the conversation.

"What did you have for supper?"

"First we had a soup," Karoline said, gesturing with her index finger as if to help her remember the different dishes. "Then we had reindeer steak with potatoes, carrots, brussel sprouts, and lingonberries. And we had ice cream with warm raspberries for dessert," Karoline finished, tapping her ring finger on her other hand by now.

"Was there anything to drink as well?"

"I had some lemonade. The grown-ups had beer."

"Did they have any napkins?"

"Oh, yes!" Karoline's eyes lit up immediately at this question. "There were these beautiful, soft, white paper napkins with pink roses stamped in the middle, and a wonderful golden frame painted along the edges."

"That sounds like a wonderful napkin," Grandma Gjertrud replied. "Really something you might want to add to your collection."

Karoline suddenly looked down at her lap and the sparkle in her eyes quickly disappeared. Grandma Gjertrud realized she was getting close to finding out Karoline's problem and tried to figure out what information to ask for next.

"Who else was at the table with you?"

Karoline took a quick extra breath. Not easy to notice, but for Grandma Gjertrud this was all she needed. She waited for the answer that might hopefully make the matter easier to understand.

"Her father was home..." whispered Karoline.

"Oh, he has been travelling a lot, hasn't he. Guess you hadn't met him before. Was he nice?"

Karoline took a new short breath and a deeper frown line formed on her forehead.

"No, he was angry. He even shouted at me when I accidentally spilled some food on the tablecloth."

By now Grandma Gjertrud was running one hand slowly up and down Karoline's back, looking into her eyes, smiling, and deliberately sending her all the love her heart could produce.

"Oh, poor Karoline, that must have made you feel really scared."

"I did my best to sort it out so there wouldn't be a stain. I even used my beautiful napkin that I had put in my pocket to bring home to mop up some of the spilled food, but he was still furious. You should have seen his eyes. They were almost black when he looked at me."

Karoline now seemed to be gasping for breath, tears forming in her eyes. Grandma Gjertrud thought to herself, "Not quite there yet…"

"What was the scariest thing about it, Karoline?"

"I don't know," whispered Karoline.

Karoline's deeper frown line and big, scared eyes still made Grandma Gjertrud think, "She knows, but cannot tell me exactly what was wrong."

Knowing there must have been more to this story, Grandma listened inward again, opened her heart and mouth, and jumped into finding the root of Karoline's distress.

"Are you perhaps afraid that your daddy might do the same when he comes home from his travels next weekend?"

Nodding slightly and by now crying heavily, Karoline threw herself into Grandma Gjertrud's arms. Bingo!

"My darling Karoline," Grandma said, gently caressing Karoline's hair. "I can assure you that is never going to happen! In *this* house, I am in charge of caring for peace and I love that job!"

Karoline's crying stopped. Her breathing became deeper and she began to relax in Grandma's arms, feeling better, but not yet fulfilled.

"Wow, is that difficult?"

"Actually, when I think about it, I wonder if you aren't just the right age to learn about taking care of peace, too. Would you like me to teach you that, Karoline?"

Karoline's face lit up in a big smile, threw herself into Grandma Gjertrud's arms, and gave her a big hug. Mission completed!

Grandma explained that it was going take awhile to learn everything about keeping the peace, and that it might even get boring sometimes along the way, but Karoline was eager to start right away. So Grandma Gjertrud, always conscious not to overdo the happenings of the day, came up with a little tiny exercise to make sure Karoline would lay her head on her pillow in a good mood and get a full night's sleep. She had Karoline lie down with closed eyes and concentrate on breathing deeply. Then she introduced the first exercise to her.

"Think of something you love doing, Karoline. I often think about going swimming, but you can choose whatever you want. Eating ice cream, picking wild strawberries, going skiing down a long hillside, jumping on your trampoline. Can you picture something now?"

"Yeah."

"Now notice the feeling of really loving it. Can you feel it?"

"Yeah, it's in my chest."

"Good girl. Now let the feeling expand as you think about what you love. Let the feeling fill all of your body."

"Oh, it makes my toes tickle!"

"Good girl!"

"Now let the feeling expand to fill your whole room. Are you okay with that?"

"Yes, Grandma." Karoline was now smiling, obviously having a good time.

"Wonderful! Now let the feeling expand to fill the whole house, and then on to fill up the whole farm. You´re doing really well, Karoline!"

"Can you see it, Grandma?"

"Yes, I can follow you with my inner eye and can see that you are very good at this. Now let´s give this feeling as a present to Mummy Hilde and your brothers, and to all the animals in the barn, the plants in the garden, and the birds in their nests. Excellent, Karoline! I can see that you are really tired now so let me help you do one last expansion. Together we will expand the feeling until we find Daddy Henrik on his travels and present it to him as well. Can you feel it?"

A deep, confident sigh revealed that Karoline was already off to sleep. Grandma Gjertrud tucked the covers gently around Karoline. She *knew* more than noticed that the atmosphere of the room was now perfect as she closed the door behind her on her way out.

Bedtime Story Number Two

The next morning Karoline showed up bright-eyed and early for breakfast with a big smile on her face. Grandma Gjertrud was standing by the stove preparing porridge, and she winked and smiled back. This secret wink confirmed they still had a deal. It showed Karoline that it was their special secret and that they wouldn't be sharing it with anyone else for the time being. Karoline felt like she hadn't eaten in a week. She served herself a big portion of porridge with lots of butter in the middle, and sprinkled roasted nuts and seeds on the top.

Karoline's mother, Hilde, was also at the table, helping Karoline's little brother, one-year-old Samuel with his breakfast.

"You seem to have had a good night's sleep," she said, blowing on a spoonful of porridge and holding it out to Samuel to gobble up.

"Oh, yes!" Karoline's face lit up with a smile. "I dreamed I was travelling with Daddy. We went to a beach and ate lots of ice cream."

"Well, that sounds like a typical thing the two of you would be doing together. By the way, did he mention when he'll be back home?" Hilde winked and laughed at Karoline.

"Oh Mummy," Karoline sighed. "I didn't really meet up with him. It was just a dream."

"Well..." Hilde nodded her head slowly, her eyes losing focus. "You never really know, do you?" she said, more to herself than to Karoline.

The morning peace was broken when Karoline's older brother, Olaf, burst into the kitchen, suddenly realizing he was running late for school.

"Don't forget your lunchbox!" Grandma Gjertrud called. "I've made your favorite – a bacon omelet with veggies." Olaf quickly turned, grabbed his lunchbox, giving Grandma Gjertrud a quick shy hug before running out the door.

"Don't I just love that boy!" Grandma Gjertrud said, nodding at Hilde. "Highly intelligent and handsome, yet still prepared to hug an old lady like me."

"He's starting to remind me more and more of my father," Hilde replied, smiling to herself.

Karoline was almost bursting with excitement by the time she finished her breakfast. She could hardly wait for her mother to go off to work leaving her alone with Grandma Gjertrud, but Hilde curled up comfortably on the kitchen couch nursing Samuel, enjoying the cozy scene before her and didn't seem to be in any hurry to rush off today.

"I can hardly remember now how I used to struggle to get all of us out of the house in the mornings when we lived in the city," she said, mostly to herself. "And it is not even three months since we moved in here with you, Grandma Gjertrud. I am so grateful to you for offering to look after the little ones this spring, making it possible for me to work part-time at the health care center. Henrik is travelling such a lot at the moment, raising money for our new barn."

"The pleasure is all mine," Grandma Gjertrud replied. Having finished her bowl of porridge, she was now enjoying her huge cup of morning tea. "What a thrill for an old lady like me to be allowed to care for a bright, wise, and clever girl like Karoline! Not to mention the little sweetie on your lap. He is already charming and even smells gorgeous. I don't suppose, by any chance, there would be another one coming?" she said, looking curiously and directly at Hilde.

"Not that I know of," Hilde replied, hiding a shy smile. "I guess that's why I am holding on to this one as long as I can, and still breastfeeding him although he is now more than a year old."

"Seems to me he's enjoying it, too," Grandma Gjertrud responded, smiling back at her and pointing at little Samuel who was now sleeping soundly in his mother's arms. "Don't see any reason why you should stop when you're both happy."

"I guess I'll put him to bed before getting ready for work. Is it okay to leave you two ladies to clear the table and do the dishes?"

"Oh, I think we can manage that." Grandma Gjertrud smiled secretly at Karoline who immediately jumped off her chair and put her bowl into the dishwasher. By the time Hilde left for work they had the kitchen all clean and shining. Karoline had even put a little tablecloth and a pot of geraniums on the kitchen table.

"Let's make a nice big pot of herbal tea and then the two of us can sit down and have a secret chat," Grandma Gjertrud said. "If I am not mistaken, we still have some cookies in the tin. Can you find us some cups and napkins, Karoline?"

An air of calm fell over the pair as they enjoyed their tea and cookies in the cozy kitchen.

"So Karoline," said Grandma Gjertrud. "What do you think I meant when I said that I was the one who took care of peace in this house?"

"You make sure that people don't ever get angry or upset," Karoline replied.

"Not quite. There's nothing wrong with feeling angry or upset. It's how you deal with those feelings that counts and how you choose to express them. I help people with that."

"But what is it that you do? How do you help the people?"

"I've learned a lot of techniques in my long life and would be happy to share them with you, but let's start with a story about how people did it in the past. I am going to tell you how people cared for peace back in the old days, Karoline. This story was passed down to me by my grandmother, who heard it from her grandmother, who heard it from her grandmother, and so on. It took place in Egypt, more than three thousand years ago, and one of my ancestors was supposedly there. Her name was Meridit."

Karoline listened intently as Grandma Gjertrud began to talk.

"In those days, people used to say that women got their strength and power by connecting with Mother Earth. Mother Earth's power, they said, was constant, cold, and calming, much like they pictured a woman to be. In the same way, they claimed that men got their strength and power by connecting to the Sun. The Sun's power was vibrant, quick, hot, and almost sticky, making men fit for tough jobs, but often leaving them rather unpleasant to be around.

Meridit lived in a town in a rural part of the country, together with her husband Omar and their two children, Tara and Ramon. The townhouses were small and close together, and the village was protected by a large wall making it possible to totally close off the town from foreign invaders. When they were threatened, the men of the village would gather and go out to make sure peace would prevail. Sometimes they had to fight, and sometimes they even had to kill those that were threatening them. They did not do it with a light heart, but they did it to make sure the families in the little village could continue to live in peace.

"When the men were fighting, they attracted more Sun-power than usual. This made them pretty hot and thoughtless. Their women would do their best to protect the men from getting too unbalanced by sewing cooling, semi-precious stones into their garments. Still, it was a well-known fact that men who went off to war would often come back in a bad state – so much so that they would not immediately be let inside the village walls when they got home. The women did not find them to be fit company for their families. As it was the women's job to keep peace at home, they would gather outside the city walls to perform a cooling-down ceremony when the men were expected home."

"But how did they know when the men would return?" Karoline couldn't help asking.

"They just knew," Grandma Gjertrud responded, continuing on with the story.

"*The men would send a message to the women through their thoughts, and when the women started to feel that message, the village came alive with all kinds of preparations. They would clean out the houses, ask the children to pick lotus-flowers, and bring out candles and incense. They'd make huge pots of stew which sent wonderful smells of meat, vegetables, ginger and garlic cooking wafting throughout the village. Washing-water was heated, shaving equipment prepared, and clean clothes laid out in front of each house.*

A little while before the men were seen on the horizon, the women would gather outside the village walls. Those men who didn't have their own woman were greeted by mothers or grandmothers, or someone living nearby as it was believed no man should be alone when returning from war. The women would stand in a circle, facing each other, knees slightly bent. Not a word was spoken, and yet every woman concentrated on the same thing. Each imagined a kind of root reaching from the end of their spine into the ground through which they could send all their worries, all the irritation, and the heat they had accumulated while dealing with family responsibilities alone. Then back up the imagined root came soothing and cooling Earth-power.

When the men drew near, the women would face each other in two rows, raising their arms in the air to make a canopy for the men to walk under as they came into the village. Laying down all their gear and weapons, the men would then walk, one at a time, through the canopy up to the village gate. During this walk, the women would use their arms to fan them with calm and soothing motions which started to transform the men from tense and savage-like to relaxed and loving.

When the cooling-ceremony was over, the women would follow their men home. To finish off the purification, the men would shave and take a bath in water scented with calming oils of lavender and rose. At last, the men were allowed inside the house to eat and be with their families. Everyone offered prayers to the God of all gods, showing appreciation for the peace, their love for each other, and the food they were about to eat. This was a memorable moment, especially for the children.

One evening in Meridit's home after the men had returned from battle, Ramon climbed into his father's lap and asked him to tell a story. Omar, his father, told of challenges that seemed almost impossible to overcome, but no matter how bad it had looked, everything turned out well in the end. In the warm and peaceful atmosphere, the children dozed off to sleep.

While Omar was telling his stories, Meridit and the other women would go back through the gate out of the city, to cool down the weapons and other gear that had been used for war. Before nightfall it would all be carried back into the village, and before settling down for the evening they would firmly close the city gate, making sure everyone would sleep safe and sound in their own beds."

It took a while before Karoline realized the story had come to an end. She was resting her head in one hand, looking out into the distance and deep inside herself at the same time. Before she could rouse herself from her reverie, Samuel had woken up and started to cry, making it perfectly clear he wanted to join them, and rather quickly too!

"What perfect timing!" cried Grandma Gjertrud. "Just as I finish my story, Samuel wakes up! What do you say we make some lunch and then the three of us can go for a walk? It's such a lovely sunny day."

"Can we go over to the playground and see if there is someone else there for me to play with?" Karoline asked, drinking the last mouthful of her tea.

"Good idea, honey," Grandma replied. She knew that learning should always be interspersed with rest, relaxation, or play, making it easier to fully incorporate what one has just heard.

When the three of them arrived at the playground, there were lots of other kids playing there. Karoline immediately saw some kids she knew and ran off to join them while Samuel was put on a sheepskin rug on the ground. He was happy to sit there throwing pine cones up into the air and watching them come down again. Grandma Gjertrud sat down on a bench facing the sun next to some other women and was lucky enough to be offered a cup of coffee. This was a whole new world for Grandma Gjertrud, who'd never had any children of her own and hadn't visited many playgrounds in her life. All the women had a good laugh together, as Grandma Gjertrud tried to figure out which child belonged to which mother, and who the other women were related to in the village. Mostly they turned out to be daughters or granddaughters of Grandma Gjertrud's old friends.

When all the others left the playground to go home, Grandma Gjertrud made no signs of wanting to leave. Karoline approached her with an eager smile.

"Can you please show me how to make a root like you were talking about?"

"I'd love to, honey," Grandma Gjertrud smiled. She was happy that Karoline had been processing her story while she'd been playing.

"Let's see if Samuel wants to join us while we hold hands and make a ring."

Samuel loved standing on his slightly uncontrollable feet, and when Grandma Gjertrud instructed the children to slightly bend their knees and bounce up and down, both he and Karoline shrieked with joy. By the time they'd finished the exercise, all three of them felt calm, relaxed, yet full of energy. Karoline couldn't wait to get home and tell her mummy all about her exciting day.

Bedtime Story Number Three

The next morning Karoline hurried to help Grandma Gjertrud clear the table and clean up the kitchen after breakfast, excited to find out what she and Grandma Gjertrud would be talking about that day. Just as she laid out the teapot and the tin of cookies on the little table, her excitement was broken by a knock on the door. In came Ingrid, their neighbor from down the road.

"It's good to see you!" Grandma Gjertrud greeted Ingrid with a big smile, as if she was not in the least surprised to see her. "Perfect timing! We are just about to sit down to have some tea. Please come and join us at the table."

Karoline could scarcely hide her disappointment at this intruder destroying her favorite time with Grandma Gjertrud, but to her surprise the normally so observant lady did not seem to notice Karoline's feelings at all. It was the visitor who broke the ice by asking Karoline how she liked living on the farm compared to living in the city.

"It is so great!" Karoline quickly replied, forgetting all about her disappointment only seconds before. "I learn new things all the time. We have already bought two sheep and they are going to have babies any day now!" Her eyes sparkled as she spoke.

"Oh, I love newborn lambs," Ingrid replied in a dreamy voice. Her eyes looked like they were filled with wonderful memories from old times. "I'd love to come to see them. Do you think you could let me know when they arrive?"

As Ingrid finished her tea she put her cup down and turned to Grandma Gjertrud. "I have a situation," she said, "and I would like to ask your advice if you don't mind."

"If there is anything I can contribute, I'd be happy to help," Grandma Gjertrud replied, trying to catch Karoline's eye. "I know we had other plans, but would you mind doing something on your own for awhile, Karoline? Read a book, maybe, or do some drawing?"

"I think I'll make a drawing or two for Ingrid," Karoline said, going into her bedroom which was next to the kitchen. Being quite curious to know what the two ladies were going to talk about, she left the door slightly open so she could eavesdrop, but she soon forgot to listen as she got caught up in her artwork.

"Ingrid is about to leave, Karoline. Would you like to come to say goodbye to her?"

Karoline was called back to reality by Grandma Gjertrud's voice. She grabbed her drawing as she left her desk and returned to the kitchen.

"This is for you," she said, giving her drawing to Ingrid. "I have put my name on it."

"How beautiful! Thank you!" cried Ingrid, and gave Karoline a warm hug. "And thank you for letting me have some time alone with your grandmother. She is a wise and mysterious woman, that one," she whispered in Karoline's ear before letting go of her.

On her way out Ingrid seemed to suddenly remember something. Turning around to Grandma Gjertrud she said, "I forgot to mention something. Mrs. Andersen has got *vaskedilla*. She is very stressed and for the past few weeks has been cleaning her house constantly, over and over again. Whenever I see her she looks exhausted and worried, just like I used to a year ago before I met you."

"Thank you for letting me know," Grandma Gjertrud said. "I guess I might be getting another visitor at some point after hearing this news."

The two ladies exchanged wise smiles and hugged each other. Just as Ingrid left, shutting the door behind her, Samuel started to cry.

"He's got perfect timing, that little brother of yours" Grandma Gjertrud said, smiling at Karoline. "Could you pick him up while I make us some lunch?"

After lunch they put Samuel in the stroller and since it was too cold to sit down over at the playground, they decided to walk to the nearby woods. They walked briskly along the country lane, cheeks rosy with effort and cold, but once inside the wooded area the cold was not as persistent so they could slow down and still keep warm.

"What did Ingrid mean when she talked about Mrs. Andersen cleaning and cleaning like that and having *vaskedilla*?" Karoline asked curiously.

"Well, isn't that a perfect question, honey," Grandma Gjertrud said, smiling at Karoline. "You are such a bright girl, able to spot an important conversation when you hear it."

Karoline felt a sudden warmth spread all over her middle and her cheeks blushed from this unusual praise.

"Can I first ask you something about this morning, Karoline?"

Karoline nodded, looking curiously back at Grandma Gjertrud.

"When Ingrid arrived this morning I could not help noticing you were a bit disappointed. What was that all about, honey?"

Karoline suddenly felt a bit shy. She looked at the tip of her shoes and hesitated before she answered, "I was afraid you would forget everything about our secret, and that I would not learn anything new today." Her voice was almost a whisper.

"I know, honey. I could quite clearly feel that in my heart. Still, as you know, I chose not to do much about it as I realized it would be a great way of learning about *perfect timing*. You see, it is always possible to find the perfect timing in everything, once you look for it. Tell me, did you have anything special you wanted us to talk about this morning?" Grandma Gjertrud asked looking inquisitively at Karoline.

"Not particularly," Karoline replied. "I just wanted to learn more from all the things that you know."

"But after our visitor left, did you have a question?"

"Yes!" Karoline responded eagerly. "I wondered what to make of the strange thing Neighbor Ingrid said about Mrs. Andersen having *vaskedilla,* and all her strange cleaning."

"This is so perfect, Karoline. Do you know what impresses me the most about this?" Grandma Gjertrud didn't wait for Karoline's reply. "You could have chosen to indulge in the feeling of disappointment, but what did you do? You started drawing which is something that you normally love doing, and soon you felt much better. Isn't that magical?"

Karoline stopped walking and thought about it for a moment, then turned to face Grandma Gjertrud. "I felt better because I thought about something that I love, even though I did not realize it at the time."

"Yes, you did," the old woman smiled back at her." You got in charge of your mood and had a good time. Then when Ingrid was about to leave you noticed something that caught your attention, so now we do have something important to talk about. You were afraid that our visitor would take away your opportunity of learning today, but quite the contrary. Our visitor was the input you needed to go on with your learning. That is what I mean by perfect timing, Karoline, and you did very well with this lesson today."

"Even Samuel let us finish before he woke up," Karoline added.

"You are perfectly right!" Grandma Gjertrud's face glowed with her smile. "I have never understood how these little ones manage to sleep exactly when they are supposed to, but I sure know how to be grateful for their perfect timing when I see it!"

"Now let's get back to your question, Karoline. You wanted to know what was all that talk about Mrs. Andersen's strange cleaning behavior – *vaskedilla*, correct?" Grandma stated as she started walking again as Samuel was starting to fidget because they were not moving anymore. "Normally when one uses the word *vaskedilla* it means that someone is washing and cleaning and tidying up much more than normal, often so much that they get totally exhausted, but still are not able to stop. When Ingrid and I were talking about Mrs. Andersen having *vaskedilla*, we actually meant something slightly different."

"Do you mean Mrs. Andersen is not really cleaning?" Karoline said looking at Grandma Gjertrud.

"No, no. She is cleaning a lot, that is for sure, but she seems to have totally forgotten WHY she is doing it," Grandma Gjertrud replied.

"But is she not doing it to make her house clean?" Karoline started to sound confused.

"Of course she is," Grandma Gjertrud assured her. "But most of all she is trying to get back the good atmosphere she used to have in her home. It's just that she seems to have forgotten how to achieve that."

"But how can you forget something that important once you have learned it?" Karoline was puzzled.

"Well," Grandma Gjertrud said, letting out a loud sigh. "To be honest, Karoline, it happens all the time. Of course, I can't go into details with you about Mrs.

Andersen's life and problems, but I can give you an example of the type of situation where I would use the word *vaskedilla* in the same way. Let's say a woman has worked in a general store for many years, working long hours, hurrying home to look after her children and cooking for the family. This has been very tiring for her. Somewhere along the way she forgets how to cool down her husband and gradually they start arguing. First the arguments are about small things like who is going to do the dishes or take out the garbage, but after awhile it gets more serious because they both become filled with hot sun-power while working so much outside the house. They say really nasty things to each other, using words they know are hurtful." Grandma Gjertrud stopped to make sure Karoline was following her explanation, then continued speaking and walking.

"One day that woman tells her husband that he is totally useless, thinking only of himself, and never contributing at home. Her husband, secretly having to admit she's right, feels hurt and becomes really angry and shouts back at her, 'Who are you to complain? You don't even manage to keep the house clean!' The woman is so hurt she starts crying, unable to utter a word. Her husband is a bit uncomfortable about making her cry, but he is certainly not prepared to admit that he is sorry. After all, she was the one who started the argument! So he turns around and leaves the room, realizing it might be best to keep out of her way for a while."

"The poor woman." Karoline could not resist breaking into the story to defend her female sister.

"Well, to be honest, I am not too sure about that, Karoline. I think they were both to blame when it comes to bad behavior. They were acting like spoiled kids, the pair of them," Grandma Gjertrud replied. "But on the other hand, when people are having problems, blaming others doesn't get you far. Helping people to start acting differently is more my style."

"But what happened to her after this, Grandma Gjertrud?" Karoline was starting to get a bit impatient.

"Inside her head our woman kept hearing her husband's voice over and over again: 'Not clean enough, not clean enough' until she didn't even notice it anymore. There was just this constant nagging feeling that she had to keep cleaning the house. Cleaning seemed very important, but she just could not remember WHY. She felt really, really bad for forgetting the reason behind the constant cleaning. She started tidying and washing as never before, but all it did was make her feel more tired and miserable. She had totally forgotten all the other things that contribute to making a good atmosphere. She even forgot to cool down her husband, not to mention cool down herself. All she knew was that she never felt she had really finished off the job and in fact, she still has not finished because she doesn't know what it is that she has forgotten."

"But Grandma Gjertrud, can't you just tell her she's finished with her cleaning?" Karoline said, eager to help.

"Of course I can, but she will have to ask me. In due time, when she is tired of being tired, she will come by to ask my advice. 'You know so much about people,' she'll say. 'Can you please advise me on what to do?' That will be the perfect time to remind her about what she has forgotten."

At that, Grandma Gjertrud was interrupted by Samuel's wails from the stroller. She and Karoline had been so caught up with their story they'd forgotten to keep walking, and Samuel had had enough of sitting still.

"And the correct reply to *this* young man is…?" Grandma Gjertrud smiled and winked at Karoline.

"Perfect timing, Samuel!" Karoline laughed as all three of them turned around and started to walk briskly back home to the warmth of their cozy kitchen.

Bedtime Story Number Four

"I'll have to do some housework while Samuel is taking his morning nap," Grandma Gjertrud announced next morning. Karoline was taken aback at her statement. She was already used to this being her secret time with Grandma Gjertrud, and she immediately felt a bit sad and rejected. Before she had time to indulge that feeling, though, she heard a careful knock on the door.

Karoline looked at Grandma Gjertrud, interested to see how she would react to someone coming to visit now that she'd planned to get some work done. Grandma Gjertrud looked back at Karoline with a smile, her eyebrows raised like she was waiting for Karoline to say something special. Puzzled at first, Karoline soon rose to the occasion. "Perfect timing!" they both said giggling before Grandma Gjertrud said in a little louder voice, "Please, come in!"

The door opened and in came Karoline's best friend, Anne, asking if she wanted to come out and play. Karoline immediately jumped up and hurried to find her warm outdoor clothes, eager to get outside as soon as possible to be with her friend. She hugged Grandma Gjertrud goodbye, quickly bent over and whispered in her ear, "I love perfect timing."

Hours later Karoline came rushing back into the kitchen with sparkling eyes and red, rosy cheeks. "Can we go over to Anne's place to play?" she asked excitedly. "Anne says I can even stay for dinner if I want to. May I, Grandma Gjertrud? Please?"

"Sure, honey," Grandma Gjertrud assured her. She popped the last tray of cookies into the over and thought to herself, *Karoline didn't seem to be scared of Anne's father anymore.*

It was bedtime before they saw each other again. Grandma Gjertrud had been out for the evening so she made a point of going in to see Karoline when she got home. She wanted to tuck her in and say goodnight, plus she was also keen to hear how dinner at Anne's house had turned out this time. As soon as she entered the room, however, she knew that Karoline had had a wonderful day and did not even need to ask about it.

"Can I ask you something now, even if it is late?" Karoline said enthusiastically.

"Perfect timing," said Grandma Gjertrud who could not resist smiling as she nodded to assure Karoline it would be okay to have some secret time now.

"Why did you say yesterday that Mrs. Andersen has to ask you before you can tell her what to do? You know so many important things and you said that you know why she is in trouble and how she could easily get out of it. So why is it not okay just to tell her that right away?"

"That is a very good question, honey," Grandma Gjertrud said. "It is very important to be able to ask the right questions. Let me answer it by telling you the story about Parzifal.

"Parzifal was a beautiful, fair-haired young man living in France about 1000 years ago. For as long as he could remember, he had heard tales of a marvelous cup called the Holy Grail. It was said that owning this cup was the best thing that could ever happen to you, and he had therefore decided to find this treasure as soon as he was old enough to leave home and search for it.

His father, a great knight, had died when Parzifal was a young boy, and since then Parzifal had lived alone with his mother. He loved her very much and tried to do what she desired of him, but there were so many things he wanted to learn: archery, riding horses, and all the things that real knights did in their daily lives. Much as his mother meant to him, what he really longed for was a father who could teach him these things.

Parzifal had always felt that he was destined to do something important when he grew up and he could hardly wait to get started.

Finally the day came when his mother said he could go out into the world to seek his fortune. Parzifal hurriedly packed up his things, full of excitement. When he was ready to leave, his mother presented him with his father's sword. 'This is yours now, my son,' she said. 'Use it well.' Blinking back tears, she added, 'I give you two pieces of advice as you set out on your journey. First, always kiss a beautiful maiden gracefully on the back of her hand, and second, whatever you do, do not bother others by asking too many questions.' Parzifal said goodbye to his crying mother and mounting his beautiful white horse he set off to see the big, wide world.

After a short day's ride Parzifal came to a grim looking castle surrounded by a wide moat. While he was still at a reasonable distance from the castle, and before he had even had time to wonder how to enter it, a fanfare of horns sounded and the drawbridge was lowered so that he could ride straight into the courtyard. Upon entering, Parzifal was greeted by the most beautiful girl he had ever seen.

Parzifal had not spent much time around beautiful girls and wasn't quite sure how he should act around one so stunning, but remembering his mother's advice, he jumped off his horse and took her hand to kiss it. However, in his confusion, he ended up kissing her squarely on her mouth. A sigh went through the crowd that had gathered to watch and two knights came rushing up with a tight grip on their swords. The girl waved them away, asked a boy to take care of the horse, and took Parzifal by the arm to show him to his room inside the castle.

'We have been waiting for you,' she said. 'Dinner is served in the Knights Hall after sunset. There you will meet the king.' Before Parzifal was able to ask any questions, the girl was gone.

He looked around the room, which was very grand. There was a huge bed in the center of the room, and off to his left side was a washbowl with warm water and clean towels. When he had washed himself thoroughly, he noticed the clean clothes lying on the bed. 'How strange,' he thought as he tried them on. 'They are just my size. How is that possible?'

When he went down into the Knights Hall later that evening the seats along the walls were already filled with people, but they sat in total silence. In the center of the room, the King was seated on his throne. It was difficult to tell his age, but his face was a greyish color and he seemed very sad. Parzifal thought the King might be ill, but remembering his mother's advice to not ask too many questions, he chose to keep his thoughts to himself. Seated next to the King was the beautiful girl who had greeted him and Parzifal paled when he realized that this girl he had kissed might actually be the Queen.

Before he had time to worry what the King might have to say about Parzifal's improper behavior, with a fanfare of trumpets the huge doors opened and in came a procession of the most beautiful youths and maidens anyone could imagine. Leading the procession was a fair-haired girl clothed in white. She carried a cup decorated with glittering jewels and Parzifal thought he had never seen anything more beautiful. The cup seemed to radiate a strong light that lit up the whole room and as Parzifal looked on, dumbfounded, he realized that this must be the Holy Grail. He wanted to ask someone if that was really possible, but was again stopped by his mother's warning. 'I can ask someone tomorrow,' he decided.

'Since I have found the right place, and they have given me a bed to sleep in, there is no rush.'

Dinner was served, and since he was seated close to the King, Parzifal could observe the sad and painful expression on the King's face.

'I wonder if the King is ill, or maybe he has lost someone he loved?' Parzifal wanted to ask the King what was the matter with him, but he refrained. He could feel deep inside his heart that something was wrong, but his mother's words made him keep his silence. 'I am a simple boy,' he thought. 'The King will find me rude if I ask.'

It was late evening before Parzifal climbed into the huge bed in his room, and he fell asleep almost before his head hit the pillow.

The next morning, he woke up to the sound of birds singing and rose to look out of the window. It was already full daylight, but no one was to be seen in the courtyard. After dressing, he went down and entered the Knights Hall, but found it empty. Upon further inspection, so was the kitchen: no fire blazing, no food cooking. 'How odd,' Parzifal thought. 'Where is *everybody?' He then went out into the courtyard and walked to the stables. His horse greeted him with a toss of his head, yet he was alone in the large stables. Neither a horse nor man could be found.*

The castle seemed like a ghostly shell of a building, and when Parzifal saw that the drawbridge was lowered, he decided to ride out and try to find people outside the castle walls. Riding as fast as his horse could go, he met no one the whole day during his travels. When darkness came, he rested his head against a tree and eventually went to sleep. How he missed the big, comfortable bed in the King's castle!

His search for people continued the next day. He did meet up with others, but they did not know of the castle and had never heard of the amazing cup. One day went by and then another. Parzifal roamed the land, asking everyone he met about what he had seen, but no one could help him solve the mystery of what he had seen in the castle. Days became weeks, weeks became months, and finally months became years. Parzifal, who had been a young man when he left home, had matured into a grown-up and responsible man.

'I should go home to my mother and do some real work,' he thought, *but he could not forget the sight of the sad King and that glowing cup. 'I must see it again! I just cannot return home before I find it!'*

One day Parzifal heard tell of a Sage who had an exceptional knowledge of many things, and before the sun had set he found the man's little cottage. Once again, he told the story of the magnificent castle, the sad King and the beautiful cup, but this time the listener nodded in recognition while Parzifal told the story.

'You have certainly been lucky, my boy,' the Sage said. 'Imagine finding the Holy Grail the very same day you set out to look for it. I know of people who have searched a whole lifetime without finding it.'

'That might be so,' Parzifal said, 'but everything was lost again to me, and now I cannot find my way back, no matter how much I search. Please tell me what to do!'

'Well,' hesitantly said the Sage. 'I don't know if it will be of any help to you, but I can tell you what happened the night you came to the castle. The girl you met in the courtyard was not the Queen, but the King's daughter, and you should have listened to your mother's advice and settled for kissing her on the hand. The King was truly both ill and sad. If you had asked, you would have learned that he was sad because he had lost one of his sons. Some more questioning and you would have discovered that this son was your own father. The fact that the King was seriously ill meant he needed someone to help him guard the Holy Grail. He was very happy that at last you had found your family so you could take on this important task.'

'Ah,' Parzifal sighed. 'Why didn't the King tell me that he was my grandfather?'

'Because he had to wait for you to ask,' the Sage answered. 'This is how the world works. If you want to know something of importance, you have to ask. The one who has knowledge cannot say anything before he or she is asked to disclose it. There needs to be an invitation, as we say. If we don't get an invitation, we have to hold our own counsel, no matter how frustrating it may be to have information that others need and not be allowed to share it.'

'But I just followed my mother's advice,' Parzifal objected.

'It may well have been good advice for your mother, but for you, it did not turn out well,' said the Sage. 'Deep down in your heart, you knew very well what to do, but for some reason you chose to listen more to your mother's voice. That was unwise. Becoming an adult is very much about finding out who you are and getting accustomed to navigating by your own Inner Voice. That way you will always know what to do in any situation.'

'Will I ever find my way back to the castle?' Parzifal asked.

'That is up to you,' the Sage answered. 'I suggest you work on listening to that Inner Voice of yours and concentrate on the image of the Holy Grail inside you while you keep searching."

"Oh no!" cried Karoline. "It can't be over yet. Please! I would have loved to have been that princess, living in such a beautiful castle and having the Holy Grail right there in front of me to gaze at every day. Do you think Parzifal would have found us both again?"

"I'm sure you can find that out in your dreams, honey," Grandma Gjertrud said, smiling at her beloved girl. "Now let me tuck you in so you get a good, deep, undisturbed sleep." Even before she had finished tucking the quilts around Karoline, Grandma Gjertrud could tell by her breathing that she was already fast asleep.

Bedtime Story Number Five

Karoline was surprised to find Grandma Gjertrud alone in the kitchen the next morning.

"Where is everybody?" she asked, rubbing the sleep from her eyes.

"Shhh. They are asleep," Grandma Gjertrud whispered back, putting a finger to her lips. "Do you think you can manage to sneak upstairs and pick up Samuel without waking Mummy or Olaf? I would love to see them get a good, long sleep now that it's Saturday and they don't need to hurry." Karoline nodded, opened the door to the hall with great care and headed upstairs very slowly, creeping as quietly as she could.

In the meantime Grandma Gjertrud prepared breakfast for the three of them. Soon the tempting smell of bacon frying, eggs cooking, baked beans simmering, and fried tomatoes with basil filled the room.

Karoline returned with Samuel half-awake in her arms and both their faces lit up with big smiles when they saw their favorite breakfast already on the table.

"A friend of mine is giving a concert over at the church this morning," said Grandma Gjertrud, serving the bacon. "I'm going to go and listen and I wondered if you and Samuel would like to join me." She looked over at Karoline, eager to see her reaction.

"Oh, I would love to come!" cried Karoline. She loved to stand out in the garden and listen to the church bells ringing out over the countryside. They gave her a funny feeling inside, tingly and happy, and the idea of being in that church with Grandma Gjertrud filled her with excitement. Hesitantly Karoline said, "But do you think that Samuel can stay quiet long enough for us to enjoy a whole concert?"

"I have been wondering about that myself," nodded Grandma Gjertrud in agreement." But then I thought if we bring his stroller, some of his favorite toys, and something to eat and drink to keep him occupied, it might work. If it doesn't, we will just have to leave, I guess. What do you think?"

"I'm sure that will work just fine!" Karoline was so excited that the three of them were actually going out together. She did wonder, though, if she ought to offer to look after Samuel and let Grandma Gjertrud enjoy her concert in peace.

Once they had all finished eating, Grandma Gjertrud turned to Karoline. "I wonder if you could help me, honey. Do you think you could change Samuel's diaper and get him dressed while I tidy up the kitchen?"

"Sure I can!" Karoline replied happily, reassured that she should definitely come along. "No problem at all. Mummy has taught me how to do it."

Karoline was great at taking care of Samuel. They laughed and giggled in the laundry room as Karoline changed his diaper, and soon they both returned to the kitchen ready to leave. Grandma Gjertrud had prepared a basket containing food, drinks, and other handy things, and she'd left a note on the kitchen table telling the others where they had gone. Now she stood waiting, basket in one hand, diaper bag in the other.

"Okay, let's go! All we need to do is figure out how to get the stroller into the car. Silly thing. I never know how to fold it properly!"

Karoline was surprised. She had never seen Grandma Gjertrud not knowing how to do things. It was a strange and unexpected occurrence, but Karoline decided that she liked the feeling of knowing there something that even wise, old Grandma Gjertrud didn't know.

"I can do it!" she said, and she felt like she grew a couple of inches as she headed for the shed to collect it. While Grandma carried Samuel to the car and strapped him in, Karoline folded the stroller and put it in the trunk.

"Thank you, Karoline!" sighed Grandma Gjertrud. "I'm so glad you decided to join me. You've been such a help this morning. I'd never have got out in time without you."

Karoline beamed from ear to ear. She was so proud to have something of value to contribute to her precious time with Grandma Gjertrud.

Thick beams of sunlight started to break through the cloudy sky, lighting up the way in front of them as Grandma Gjertrud drove along the main road to town. The car soon started to warm up and Karoline, who was sitting next to Samuel in the back seat, leaned back, shut her eyes, and breathed in the relaxing, quiet atmosphere. Soon she could tell by the shift in his breathing that Samuel was sleeping, and she started to remember last night's story about Parzifal. Something was puzzling her, something she could not remember. At first she thought it must have been a fleeting memory from last night's dream, but that didn't seem to be it. Since she still could not remember, she started to sum up the story itself. Suddenly, there it was – her question for today. The one she had wanted to ask Grandma Gjertrud as she woke up this morning.

"Grandma Gjertrud?"

"Yes, honey?"

"Parzifal had to learn the importance of listening to his own Inner Voice, but how can I learn to listen to my own when I don't know what it sounds like?"

"That is a very important question," Grandma Gjertrud replied. "To be honest, a lot of grown-ups don't find the time to ask themselves that question during their entire lifetime. That means you can really be proud to have sorted it out so quickly, Karoline!"

Karoline started to feel a bit awkward. She did not see the search for questions to ask Grandma Gjertrud as anything special and she was beginning to get impatient for the answer." But how can I actually learn it, Grandma Gjertrud?" she persisted.

"Well," began Grandma, "Your Inner Voice is there all the time. It is a part of you that is very competent and wise, and it knows what is right and what is wrong for you. Very often though, people don't like what they hear and start to override their Inner Voice with logic, just like Parzifal did. When the Inner Voice gets rejected like this, over and over again, it stops telling you things. If you want it to start talking to you again, you will have to be patient and take the voice seriously – if you can manage to make it talk to you again." Grandma Gjertrud stopped to think. She could feel she was beginning to get a bit off track and had the impression that Karoline did not quite understand what she was trying to explain to her.

"Can it be dangerous to listen to the Inner Voice?" Karoline asked.

"Yes, it actually can," Grandma Gjertrud replied. "That is why I am struggling to find the best way to explain it to you."

"In what way can it be dangerous?" Karoline seemed a bit worried at the direction the conversation was taking.

"Some people experience what they call Inner Voices giving them commands to do strange things, maybe even dangerous and violent things. This is not the true Inner Voice I'm talking about, but it can be hard to tell the difference sometimes. That is why we need to be *absolutely sure* that we open up to our Inner Voice in a safe way. For you that means starting to learn how to tell what you love from what you don't like."

"How do I do that?" asked Karoline, sounding surprised.

"I suggest you make a list of at least ten, maybe fifteen, things that you like or even love to do. If you find it hard to write, you can always make small drawings to remind you." Grandma Gjertrud stopped talking in the middle of her explanation as she had to use all her attention to find an empty parking space in the parking lot opposite the church.

"I'm sorry, honey. It seems like we will have to talk more about this later. Is that okay with you?"

"Sure!" Karoline answered. She had already spotted the queue of people outside the church waiting to get into the concert, and she was eager to join them. She got the stroller set up again and Grandma Gjertrud managed to move Samuel into it without waking him.

As Karoline waited for Grandma Gjertrud to finish putting Samuel in his stroller, the two great church bells started ringing. "Grandma Gjertrud, listen!" Samuel woke up and blinked sleepily, but Karoline just stood and gazed up at the tower, entranced by the majestic sound. The bells ringing seemed so much louder here than it did hearing them from the farm. She could feel her chest vibrate with the great, rhythmical booming of them and the sound seemed to fill her and the whole world. "Ding, dong! Ding, dong!" The bells seemed to be talking to each other, and Karoline felt she could almost understand them. After what seemed a long time she started to feel a bit dizzy. Grandma Gjertrud touched her shoulder. "It's time to go in to the concert, honey," she said.

Grandma Gjertrud found a seat in the back of the church where she could easily fit Samuel's stroller in between herself and the wall. She pointed to the far left of the stage at the front of the church and whispered, "The lady over there is my friend, Julie. She's a violinist and the first piece she's going to play today is *Air* by a German composer called Bach. Her colleague will play the organ up in the balcony above us. You can go up nearer the front if you would like to get a better view. Remember," she added, "that if you get bored, you can always sneak back here again during a break between two tunes."

"Okey dokey!" Karoline replied. She could see some children sitting on the stairs leading up toward the platform in front of the altar and felt like joining them.

Gradually everyone settled down and the whole church was quiet. As soon as Julie started playing, Karoline felt as if the music made her smile inside, and when the organ joined in, slowly at first but gradually increasing in sound, she could feel the stairs vibrating under her. She noticed she almost felt as if she was trembling inside, too. She closed her eyes and let her upper body move slowly, feeling the music with all her senses. One of the pieces of music made her feel like she was running in a large field of flowers, her arms stretched out to each side, with the wind in her hair and laughter in her breath. Another piece made her picture herself jumping easily from cloud to cloud, having fairy wings and playing with a little dragon that invited her to sit on his back. He was flying her through magical loops and swings, making her giggle from deep within, although not a sound was heard by the children sitting close by. A more quiet piece made her hug her knees and sway softly from side to side, looking deep into herself, as if she could see mystical beings floating by, one by one, at a slow pace.

It wasn't until a twenty minute break was announced that she realized she was feeling rather hungry and cold. When she tried to get up, she felt totally stiff, as if she had not used her body for a long time. Karoline made her way towards the back and found Grandma Gjertrud smiling with Samuel on her lap. He was sucking happily on a dry cracker and Karoline went over to see if there might be a couple of crackers left for her, too.

"I have a couple of sandwiches for you, if you are hungry," Grandma Gjertrud said, much to Karoline's surprise.

"Did you make them for me?" she said, curiously.

"Of course, honey. I always get hungry when I go somewhere so I thought you might feel the same" Grandma Gjertrud said, giving Karoline a sandwich. "Before I forget, I must say that I was really proud of you when I saw you sitting there all on your own, knowing nobody. You seemed to enjoy listening to the music. Did you like it?"

"I loved it!" Karoline was having difficulty talking as her mouth was filled with food, but Grandma Gjertrud could easily tell her little girl had been enjoying the music as much as she had herself. "How about you stay back here with me after the break?" she said. "If Samuel decides he's had enough and we have to leave, we'll disturb fewer people if we're sitting here closer to the door."

"That's okay with me," Karoline said, reaching for another sandwich. She looked around to find a seat and saw several small tables with chairs around them. Each table was set with paper and colored pencils so that children could draw during services if they were bored. She looked at Grandma Gjertrud then back at the tables and whispered, "Do you think that I could work on my list while the concert is going on?"

"What a splendid idea!" smiled Grandma Gjertrud. "Perfect timing!"

It was another hour before the concert was finished and they had packed all their belongings into the car, ready to return to the farm. Samuel fell asleep on their way back home giving the other two plenty of time to discuss Karoline's list. She had managed to come up with twelve things that she loved doing:

1. Learning new things from Grandma Gjertrud
2. Listening to music

3. Drawing in my own little book
4. Playing with Anne
5. Listening to audiobooks
6. Taking a bubble bath
7. Watching videos
8. Dancing
9. Baking cakes and cookies
10. Singing
11. Going swimming
12. Being tucked into bed at night

"This is really great!" Grandma Gjertrud sounded impressed when she had heard Karoline read her all the points on the list. "When we get home, you can put up the list in your room or on the kitchen wall. Then you can start testing each point by actually doing it and see if you like each thing as much as you think you do. That will give you a way of getting to know your Inner Voice. I promise you, we will get back to the art of developing your Inner Voice when you get older, honey. Please remind me should I forget it longer than you think is suitable. Will you promise me that?"

"Sure thing . . . ," Karoline hesitated before she finished her sentence. "And when I get home I want to test point number six by taking a bubble bath."

Grandma Gjertrud smiled to herself as she drove into the driveway and decided she would make a check mark on her own list when she got back to her room that evening. Grandma Gjertrud's *Point #10: Going to concerts,* was still a valid point on her list.

Bedtime Story Number Six

The kitchen was empty and quiet as Karoline helped herself to a couple of sandwiches from the fridge the next morning. In her family, Sunday morning was "do-as-you-please" time, meaning they could all do as they wanted as long as they did not make too much noise or wake each other. Karoline poured herself a glass of juice to go along with the sandwiches and returned to her room with her breakfast. She had plans on how to spend this day. She intended to study her list from yesterday to make sure she had gotten it right and maybe find some more points to add as well. On her desk a new list was developing. She had already written two column titles with large, uneven letters LOVE and SURE at the tops of each of them. The new list had a *Point One,* already filled in. It was a drawing of lots of circles in different sizes, her image of what a bubble bath looked like to her. After having spent a whole hour in the bathtub with lots of bubbles the day before, she was certain that this was something she loved doing.

Karoline picked up her list and looked for some new points that could easily be tested on a Sunday morning. Listening to music? *Too noisy.* Drawing in my own little book? *Too boring right now.* Playing with Anne? *Too early.* Listening to an audiobook? *Takes too much time, which means I won't get to test much more this morning.* Watching videos? *Same reason as before.* Dancing? *Too much noise.* Baking cakes and cookies? *Tempting, but not allowed to use the oven if there are no grown-ups around.* Singing? *Too noisy.* Karoline stopped. She suddenly remembered that she had been singing loudly in the bath last night out of pure joy and she'd had a great time. Could she add *Singing* to the SURE list? She immediately nodded to herself and drew a couple of music notes coming out of a bird's beak as *Point Two* on her new list.

Karoline couldn't help but feel a bit disappointed while she finished eating her breakfast. She had been looking forward to bragging to Grandma Gjertrud about how many points she'd tested this morning and now she wouldn't be able to do that. As she looked around her room to find a solution, her eyes stopped at her princess dress, hanging from a cardboard box she had turned into a castle some weeks ago. "Oh!" she muttered to herself. "How could I forget to put *playing princess* on the list?" With a big smile on her face, she drew a little princess on the list and gave it the number 13. Then she hurried over to the castle to put on her princess dress.

A little while later she heard Grandma Gjertrud call out from the kitchen, "Don't forget Uncle Bernt is coming for lunch! "He'll be here any minute. Who's going to set the table before he gets here?"

Uncle Bernt was an old friend of Grandma Gjertrud's, and Olaf and Karoline always loved his visits.

Karoline immediately jumped up from the game she'd been playing and ran downstairs. "Uncle Bernt is so much fun, Grandma Gjertrud!" she cried, skipping her way into the kitchen and giving Grandma Gjertrud an enthusiastic good-morning hug. "He knows such a lot of strange things. I hope he will stay long."

Grandma Gjertrud smiled and hugged her back, noticing that Karoline was wearing her princess dress. "I can see you have been busy this morning, honey, or maybe should I call you Princess Karoline?" Karoline grinned.

"We will need plates, glasses, knives and forks for five people, plus Samuel's stuff, of course. Then we need wine glasses for three grown-ups and I would love it if you could fold some nice napkins for us. You can choose whatever type you like from the cupboard." Grandma

Gjertrud talked quickly as she stirred scrambled eggs in the frying pan and sliced smoked salmon.

"Anybody home?" shouted Uncle Bernt from the hallway. Karoline raced out to greet him just as Olaf came sliding down the bannister and they both ran straight to Uncle Bernt at the same time. Laughing, he scooped them up, one under each arm, and carried them into the kitchen.

"Where's my girl?" he said, grinning at Grandma. Freeing his arms from hugging the children he crossed the kitchen floor in two large steps and gave her a big hug. "You are as pretty as ever, Gjertrud!" he said, beaming at her.

Grandma Gjertrud blushed and looked down at her feet with a shy smile on her face. As Uncle Bernt let go of her, she hurried to smooth out any wrinkles on her apron with both hands. Uncle Bernt was the only one to notice and he shook his head, and still smiling walked over to the table to sit down.

"Olaf, can you run upstairs to let Mummy know lunch is ready?" Grandma Gjertrud said as soon as she felt sure her voice would come out sounding normal.

"Sure!" Olaf had already found a seat close to Uncle Bernt, but he hurried upstairs and soon came down a bit more slowly, carrying Samuel in his arms.

Nobody wanted to leave the table after lunch. The children were waiting for Uncle Bernt to start telling them stories of some of the strange things he'd read about during his long life. He had been a sailor and there had been plenty of time for reading on his voyages. However impatient they were though, they both knew they were not allowed to hurry things. Before he would say a word, Uncle Bernt always insisted on having his cup of specially brewed dandelion and chicory coffee that only Grandma Gjertrud could make him.

As soon as he emptied his cup, even before it had hit the saucer, Olaf had his first question ready. "Please Uncle Bernt, can you tell us some more about the flying saucers?"

"I'd love to, my boy." Uncle Bernt rearranged himself on the seat, leaning forward to rest his head on his elbows. He hesitated for a moment and then started to speak.

"Flying saucers are not something new to this planet," he said slowly, as if searching for the right words.

"There are many strange, ancient stories that tell of people visiting us from other planets. For many years I thought these were just fairy tales, but lately I have read many books claiming to more or less prove that flying saucers really exist. There is, for instance, a place in South America where huge signs have been detected on top of a mountain plateau, signs that can only be seen fully from the sky. The strange thing is that these signs are so old nobody could ever have flown that high in those days – unless..." Uncle Bernt stopped to take a deep breath. "Unless seen from a flying saucer," he finished to gasps of excitement from Olaf and Karoline.

"Personally I love the stories claiming the Egyptian Pharaohs were actually sons of God-like creatures from the star Sirius, coming to our planet in flying saucers. They were said to have extraordinary knowledge of energy and could alter gravity to suit their own needs. A practical tool when building pyramids, I guess," Grandma Gjertrud said, smiling at the thought.

"No wonder you like the Egyptian stories, *jenta mi*," Uncle Bernt smiled back at her "Tied as you are to your former life experiences from that culture."

"I have always been fascinated by the stories of Atlantis as well," Hilde added. "Weren't there claims that the people of Atlantis also knew how to use flying saucers?"

"Unless I'm mistaken, I believe they actually knew how to move matter with their thoughts. It's called telekinesis, just like they used in the Star Wars movies and other films," Uncle Bernt corrected her. "But I think that's enough flying saucer stories for one day. Anyone have a different question?" Uncle Bernt looked deliberately at Karoline giving her an opportunity to choose the next topic.

"Um ..." she said, a bit shy at first. "I would like to hear more about the plant studies you told us about last time. I could hardly believe it when you said that plants can actually respond to us."

"You are absolutely right, my Princess," Uncle Bernt said. "So much interesting work has been done showing us that plants respond both to our thoughts and to our behavior. For instance, scientists have been able to show that plants seem to remember if you cause them harm. Quite amazing! And I read the most exciting article the other day. It was about a study where two people were given identical plots of land side by side, same type of seeds, same fertilizer, same amount of water, and spent the same amount of time caring for their plants. What they wanted to know was whether or not there was a difference in the size of the harvest. I ask you, my Princess, do you think it is possible that the two people had a large difference in between their two harvests?" Uncle Bernt looked at Karoline to see her reaction. She felt uneasy, and wriggled in her seat trying to decide what to answer.

"I don't know," she finally whispered.

"Well, that is a good answer, my Princess, because the scientists did not know either, but I can tell you they were all very surprised when they discovered there was a huge difference between the two crops. First they claimed one of the participants must have cheated, but as they had made great efforts to protect against this practice they decided that was not what had happened. Would you like me to reveal the secret to you?" Uncle Bernt paused and looked at Karoline and Olaf.

"Yes!" they both shouted.

"Well … It turned out one of the people had made photographs of his field and later of his plants.

When he got home from work, he would look at the photographs, sending the plants love and encouragement and praying for them to thrive. He would also communicate with the plants while he was working in the fields, talking to them and sending them positive thoughts. His plants seemed to appreciate this as they grew bigger and healthier than the plants in the other field, and as I have told you already, his harvest was also much better than the other farmer's yield."

"I wish I had my own plant to experiment on," Karoline sighed, mainly to herself.

"If you want to, I can help you grow one," Grandma Gjertrud whispered to her, winking as she did to signal they could do this together in their secret time.

"Time for me to hit the road again," Uncle Bernt said suddenly, rising from the table. Although both children begged him to stay longer, he just gave them a hug, turned around and was gone almost before they could notice him leaving the room.

"Why does he always have to leave so quickly?" Olaf complained.

"Uncle Bernt has been alone all his life, belonging to nobody," Grandma Gjertrud answered softly. "I guess that's why he spent most of his life at sea. It seems to me he sometimes feels too crowded in parties like this and he has to get back to being on his own for a while. But I'm sure you can all tell he loves you very much. I know he appreciates my coffee," she added, "So I bet it won't be long until we get to see him again."

Later that afternoon Grandma Gjertrud took Karoline out to the greenhouse to see her geraniums. She had already moved them from their cold winter storage into the light and heat, getting them ready for spring planting. Now she showed Karoline how she could make new plants by taking cuttings from the original stems. With a sharp knife she removed some of the new shoots, took off the bottom leaves, and put the rest in a glass of water. "These cuttings will soon grow new roots and make their own plants," she explained. "You can have these two, and when their roots are large enough I will show you how to plant them in a pot. These ones are such a pretty pink color, I'm sure you will like them. If you treat them well, they can stay with you for many years."

"I will be sure to talk nicely to both of them," Karoline said, holding the glass containing her two cuttings like it was precious gold.

"I know you will, honey," Grandma Gjetrud smiled. "I understand you might want to have them in your room, but I think they will be better off here in the greenhouse, where the combination of light and temperature is better for them right now. I will be working here a lot the next few weeks, so you will have plenty of time to care for them here."

"Sure," Karoline said. "Still I think I will ask Mummy to take a photograph of them for me to have in my room."

Grandma and Karoline grabbed their coats tighter around them as they walked through the evening wind back to the house.

Bedtime Story Number Seven

There was no doubt at the breakfast table the next morning that this was going to be a special day. Everybody was smiling and their eyes were sparkling with anticipation. Olaf and Karoline were getting along like friends and even Samuel was perfectly happy sitting in his baby chair, trying to hit his mouth with a spoon full of porridge. The atmosphere had an excitement to it that made them all talk hastily, breaking into each other's conversations.

"What time is Daddy coming home?" Karoline asked.

"I'm picking him up at the airport this afternoon ..." Mummy Hilde started to answer, but Olaf couldn't wait for her to finish. "Can I come with you? Please?"

"I'm sorry, sweetheart, but the answer is no. You have to stay home and help Grandma Gjertrud prepare for Daddy's homecoming celebration. We'll be back in time for dinner." Hilde squeezed Olaf's hand and smiled at him. "You're such a big boy now. There's a lot that needs to be done and Grandma Gjertrud can really use your help."

Olaf looked glumly down at the table. It was clear he was disappointed, but he didn't have much time to worry about it because he discovered he was running late for school again.

"Don't forget your lunch box, Olaf!" Grandma Gjertrud hurried over to the door where Olaf was quickly putting on his boots. "There's a special treat in there today, to thank you for helping me this afternoon," she smiled at him while handing him his lunch box. Olaf grinned and gave her a hug, shouting goodbye as he ran out the door. "See you this afternoon!"

Hilde lifted Samuel onto her lap to nurse him before going to work. "I love your idea of taking a special bath before I go to get Henrik," she said to Grandma. "In fact, I've arranged to come home early today so I can do just that!" She grinned at Grandma.

"Good! I'm delighted to hear that," Grandma replied. "I was hoping that Karoline might help me make some cleansing bath salts for all of us this morning."

"Oh, I'd love to!" Karoline had been listening in on their conversation and was thrilled at the direction things were taking.

As soon as breakfast was over they tidied the kitchen as usual, settled Samuel for his morning nap, and enjoyed their daily herbal tea and cookies. When they were done, Karoline cleared away the tea cups while Grandma Gjertrud fetched the things they needed from the attic to make the bath salts. She came back with her arms full of boxes and bags. "Okay!" she said, putting the things down on the table and looking a little flushed. "Let's see what we've got here. This is Dead Sea salt, this is regular sea salt, and this is Epsom salt," she said, sorting out the bags.

"But isn't salt just salt? Why do they have all these names?" Karoline asked with a perplexed look on her face.

"Salt can contain lots of different ingredients, minerals we call them, depending on where it comes from. Mostly their names will tell you something about them. Dead Sea salt is made of water from the Dead Sea, which is actually a big lake. Sea salt is made from evaporated sea water. Epsom salt originally came from the town of Epsom in England where they have a spring of special water that contains both magnesium and sulfur in a combination called magnesium sulfate. I only have three types of salt here, but I could easily think of more. There's salt from Iceland which contains minerals from all the volcanoes there, and special pink salt from great mines in the Himalayas. I'm sure there must be lots of other locally produced salts around the world, all as special and individual as the places they come from."

"But why do we use these salts for bathing?" Karoline was beginning to feel overwhelmed.

"The use of salt in baths goes way back in time. In the olden days, people used to *valfarte* or make a pilgrimage to places where the water was thought to have special healing qualities because of salts that were dissolved in it. It could be warm water coming directly out of the ground, water found in caves deep inside mountains, or water from a lake, like the Blue Lagoon in Iceland. Many people felt better and stronger after bathing in the water. Seriously ill and depressed patients saw remarkable improvements in their conditions, skin diseases cleared up, and so on. So many people started coming to these special places that gradually tourist resorts grew up around the salt baths. Occasionally people drank the water, but usually such holy waters have only been used externally."

"Why? Are the different salts not safe to eat?" Karoline asked.

"Well, anything can be dangerous for your body if you eat too much of it. Even too much cooking salt can be bad for us. What I really mean though is that different salts contain different combinations of chemicals. The salt we mean when we say, 'Pass me the salt, please,' at the table will be some kind of cooking salt, and all cooking salts contain sodium and chloride, but in chemistry many other combinations of things are also known as salts. Remember I told you that Epsom salt contains sulfur and magnesium?"

"So we want to add bathing salt to our baths to make us feel better?" Karoline was getting a bit impatient. Chemistry was not so interesting when Grandma Gjertrud still had more boxes and bags, and even a couple of bottles that they had not yet looked into to see the contents.

"You are so right, honey. We want to feel better so let's get started."

Grandma Gjertrud used a measuring cup and combined different amounts of the three salts into one bigger jar. She put on the lid and asked Karoline to shake the contents until they were well mixed. Next she opened a container of ready-made bath salts from her favorite shop and added some of that to the jar too. The lid was put on again and Karoline went on shaking.

"Oh, this smells lovely!" Karoline had removed the lid on the store bought jar and had put her nose in to smell the contents.

"It's rose, lavender and something that I don't know!" laughed Grandma Gjertrud." My favorite smells! Do you think your Mummy will like it too?"

"I hope so," Karoline said hesitantly." At least I know I will!"

"I wonder if we should make another batch with a special, more masculine scent for the boys," Grandma Gjertrud said looking thoughtful.

"Oh, yes!" Karoline replied. "But what should we add to make a masculine smell?"

"That is a good question, honey!" Grandma Gjertrud smiled at Karoline. "I have some bottles of essential oils here. Let's take a look, or should I say smell, at some of the contents."

They both sniffed their way through the bottles and ended up adding some drops of rosemary in combination with pine, topped with a tiny amount of lavender to the salt mixture. Before they had time to plan yet another batch, they could hear Samuel talking to himself in his crib.

"Perfect timing," Karoline laughed, proud that she managed to say it before Grandma Gjertrud got the chance.

"Right again, Karoline," the old lady replied. "I guess if we hurry with the tidying up, we will be able to finish before he shifts to the 'I need attention right now!' end of his repertoire of babbling."

So they packed up all the boxes and bags plus the bottles of new bath salts they created, and cleared the kitchen table before starting to make lunch.

After eating their lunch, they all went for a quick walk into the woods. The sky was a bit cloudy, but the temperature was nice for this time of the year.

"I wondered if we should pick something to decorate the dinner table with to make it special," Grandma Gjertrud said. "There are no flowers out yet, but I was thinking we could make something pretty with green pine branches." Karoline nodded slightly, and Grandma could see that she was already thinking what to make out of the boughs. She didn't say any more on their walk home.

At 3:30 pm when Olaf got home from school, he found his sister deep in concentration, tying red paper hearts to a bunch of green pine branches in a big vase. She was using gold colored thread, and the effect was very pretty. Grandma Gjertrud was busy preparing the *stifado*, her favorite Greek casserole, for dinner.

"Hello, darling," she smiled." Would you like something to eat?"

Olaf, who seemed always to be hungry, slumped into one of the kitchen chairs and ate the leftovers from lunch that was put in front of him with great delight.

"Anybody home?" They heard Hilde shouting from the hall and Karoline and Olaf both jumped up and ran to greet her. They all sat down at the kitchen table. Karoline poured tea for everyone while Grandma Gjertrud found a note pad and pencil and started to write a list of all the work that had to be done before their father arrived home.

"Okay everyone. All the rooms need to be vacuumed, dusted, and cleaned, and the garbage cans need to be emptied. I need someone to set the table and fold napkins nicely, and when all that is done, we need someone to walk around the house with the little bell and someone to walk carrying the incense burner. And we shouldn't forget to have our baths! Who wants to do what?"

"I'll do the vacuum cleaning," Olaf volunteered, "And then I can set the table if you want."

"Great! You always do such a good job of the vacuuming, Olaf. Thank you," Grandma Gjertrud replied.

Karoline offered to take out all the garbage, fold the napkins prettily, and walk around the house with the incense. Hilde chose to clean the bedrooms and bathroom before curling up in her special salt bath, and Grandma Gjertrud was happy to do the rest.

The children bustled off to start their jobs and Hilde stretched in her chair and drank the last of tea. "You know," she said, "I'm a little nervous about seeing Henrik after all this time. Isn't that silly?"

"No, I don't think it's silly at all," Grandma Gjertrud replied. She hesitated. "I have a few suggestions that may help, if you're interested in hearing them."

Hilde nodded, so Grandma told her the story of Meredit, and suggested ways that she might prepare herself for meeting her husband again after so long. As she talked, Samuel fell asleep on his mummy's lap, so they laid him safely in his crib and got on with their work.

An hour or two later, the house was gleaming. Hilde breezed down the stairs with the scent of lavender and rose wafting behind her, and kissed them all as she left for the airport to pick up Henrik.

Karoline had her bath next, but Olaf preferred to have a shower. Grandma Gjertrud explained to him how he could also use the bathing salts in the shower, by first washing himself with soap and then taking some of the salts in his hand and rubbing them all over his body before rinsing it off with water. "It tickles a bit, but it smells good!" he shouted through the bathroom door much to Grandma Gjertrud and Karoline's amusement.

The last step was the cleansing the house with the ringing of the bell and the burning of incense. Grandma

Gjertrud jingled the bell in every corner of the house and showed Karoline how to light the dried herbs and walk slowly and thoroughly around the house with it, wafting the smoke into every corner of every room with a feather. It was quite magical how the feeling in the house changed as they did this, leaving a warm and comforting atmosphere behind them.

"Are you worried at all, Karoline, about your father returning home?" Grandma Gjertrud wanted to make certain that Karoline had recovered from her bad experience at Anne's house.

"How do you mean?" Karoline was confused by Grandma's question.

"You know, how we talked about you being scared that Daddy might get angry at the dinner table when he first comes home, just like Anne's father."

"Oh... that," Karoline sighed. "I didn't even think about that until you mentioned it. I am so glad you know how to take care of peace, Grandma Gjertrud, and I am proud that you're teaching me how to do it too."

Grandma Gjertrud gave Karoline a warm hug. "You have real talent for this, honey. You're going to be quite an expert at caring for peace by the time you're a grown-up. Nothing is going to get you out of balance so much you won't be able to find your center again easily."

As the smell of dinner cooking drifted through the house, three happy, warm, clean children snuggled up together on the sofa to watch a cartoon while they waited for their parents to arrive home from the airport. Grandma Gjertrud quietly shut the living room door behind her and went up the stairs to have her own bath. It was going to be good to have the whole family together again.

Grandma Gjertrud's Second Visit

Karoline's Life at Thirty-Six

Karoline sprinkled a handful of lavender scented bath salts into the steaming water in her bathtub and breathed in deeply. She smiled to herself. It had been a good week, all things considered. The comfort of hearing a bedtime story every night for a whole week had done her good. She had been sleeping better and found that she had more energy during the day. She had reintroduced tea and cookies into her daily routine and started to take brisk walks in the afternoon. She had enjoyed playing with the peace exercises.

Tonight she was expecting Grandma Gjertrud to come back, and she could hardly wait! Karoline had cleaned her flat from top to bottom, burnt her incense, and now she was ready for her special salt bath.

Later that evening Karoline sat up in bed with her knees to her chest, all her senses on alert for the light she'd seen last week. Suddenly a light glinted off the church bell and there was Grandma Gjertrud, coming across the room and sitting on her bed. Karoline relaxed and smiled.

"So I have actually misinterpreted the incident with Anne's family all these years?" Karoline had been chatting to Grandma about all she had learned the past week. "The reprimand Anne's father gave me wasn't really the problem. The real one was that I was afraid my own father might reject me and behave in the same frightening way. It wasn't the incident itself that scared me so much as how I applied the knowledge I gained from it to my own life?"

"You are so right," Grandma Gjertrud smiled. "It often boils down to us being scared that someone will reject us or withdraws their love and leaves us alone, excluded from our community."

In the first seven stories, I've tried to tell you that you, and only you, are responsible for how you feel and react to things. Other people cannot make you feel a certain way unless you let them. You are always in control. But even more important is to understand that people's actions can often be understood and predicted if we take a moment to think about things. For instance, do you understand now why Anne's father was so cross with you, and why in the story I assured you that your father would not react the same way?"

"No, not really," Karoline said.

"When Anne's father came home, he had been away from his family for quite a while. While he was away he had been working long hours, hardly speaking to anyone, and missing his loved ones. By the time he returned home he was tired, frustrated, and the last thing he needed was his daughter's friend at dinner. No wonder he was so easily annoyed! I have always strived to bring peace into people's lives by helping them to let go of their frustrations and recover a sense of inner balance. When you were little, your mother and I prepared for your father's return home from work, making sure to cool him down before he got home. This is what I mean when I talk about caring for peace at home. We never thought of letting you know at the time and that's why you got so scared of Anne's father. In these stories I have tried to include you and your brothers in all the preparations. We should probably have done that at the time. I'm sorry."

Karoline was amazed. She felt she had learned such a lot although only a few days had passed since Grandma Gjertrud had appeared in her room so unexpectedly.

"Was there anything else that you wanted help with, honey?" Grandma Gjertrud asked carefully.

"My work isn't going too well either." Karoline started to feel tense as soon as she said the words. "I still work as a teacher and I love working with the kids. I feel I understand them well and that I am able to help them achieve their full potential. Both my pupils and their parents often tell me that they love what I do and the way I do it. Lately though, I have had a new boss and he's been picking on me right from the word go, complaining about the way I write my journals and so on. First I tried to shrug his comments off by being firm and standing my ground, but after a while it really started to wear me down. Now I don't know what to do. He doesn't seem to like me at all and uses any opportunity to make me look bad. He makes me feel so wrong: so odd, and out of place. He makes me feel different from the other teachers and I've been feeling very isolated at work. I have even started to wonder if he might be right. Maybe I'm not a good teacher at all. I certainly don't seem to work like the others do."

"Have you ever felt like this before?" Grandma Gjertrud asked.

"Oh yes!" Karoline answered, no doubt in her voice. "I tend to meet those kinds of people. They don't seem to have a clue as to who I am or what I'm doing, but they are still convinced I need to change and be more the way they want me to be."

"Has it always been like that?" Grandma Gjertrud had a feeling she was honing in on something important.

"No. I remember when I was about twelve I felt I could handle anything." Karoline's voice was firm and strong, and it was clear that she was talking about something she felt happy about. "I could find solutions to problems. I could make the things I wanted to with huge success, both at home and at school. I loved bending rules and always managed to get away with it. I was extremely creative in many areas, sort of a multitasker, although I never heard anyone use that expression at the time."

"What happened?" Grandma Gjertrud asked her, sensing something important was going to be brought up.

"Something happened when I was around thirteen and went to a new school," Karoline said hesitantly, searching for the right words, but then she seemed to remember her teenage years more clearly. "It was like things were tightening up around me. Teachers wanted more from me at school and friendships got more complicated. Where earlier we would all play together, now you had to belong to someone, be someone's favorite – like have a boyfriend, a really close friend, or be in a group. At the new school I met a group of really nice kids and I loved spending time with them. We did so many cool things together and they made me feel great, but my best friend, Anne, got really hurt when I didn't spend as much time with her as I used to do. She cried and said I had to choose between her and the group. I got really frustrated, but I didn't want to hurt my best friend: we'd known each other for years and we'd always had fun together. I started joining her as she went to see her new friends. She would even ask me to come with her when visiting guys she had a crush on, but was too shy to see on her own. I was talkative, funny, and entertaining when she needed me to be. In time she became more confident and I ended up being quite silent, just supporting her by being there.

"But what was it about the group you liked?" Grandma Gjertrud asked. "Did they continue to invite you to their outings?"

"Anne made me tell them I preferred to be with her."

"But honey, was that really how you wanted things to be?" Grandma Gjertrud seemed puzzled as she asked Karoline the question.

"I don't know," Karoline said hesitantly. "People kept telling me that it was a good thing to stand up for my friends when I was a teenager and so I did. I thought it was the right thing to do and I was proud of sticking to my decision, even if it was hard at times."

"This must have been going on while I was on my painting holiday in France," Grandma Gjertrud said. "You remember, the one your parents gave me for my birthday that year."

Karoline nodded. "Yes, and when you came home I was in the middle of choosing sides, and you all seemed to think that being loyal was the right thing to do." Karoline's voice was beginning to sound unsteady and Grandma Gjertrud could sense how sad Karoline still felt about this.

"Oh, honey. I remember finding your door locked when I came to say goodnight the evening after I arrived home from that trip. I thought you just needed some time on your own, what with being a teenager and everything. I am so sorry I didn't understand your problem at the time! You must have felt extremely lonely and probably quite sad, too. Actually I think this might have some connection to the way your problems at work have developed. Would you like for us to do another seven evenings of bedtime stories and have a look at these feelings?"

"Yes please!" Karoline said eagerly. "I desperately need some help with this one."

"Great! Then I will start sending you bedtime stories tomorrow," Grandma Gjertrud said.

"But can I ask you to tuck me in tonight, too, please?"

"Any time, honey," Grandma Gjertrud replied, and she started humming while Karoline lay down and made herself comfortable, ready to be tucked in safe and warm.

PART TWO

Karoline's Life at Thirteen

Bedtime Story Number Eight

The late September sun was still warm as Grandma Gjertrud made her way out of the airplane. She loved travelling, but after spending four weeks in southern France she was delighted to be back at her local airport further north. Remembering there would be someone there to pick her up made her smile. So many blessings had sprung from her decision years ago to invite a whole family into her life, letting them move into her farmhouse with her. Always being picked up at the airport was just one of those blessings. "There she is!" Karoline shouted from behind the big windows.

"Grandma Gjertrud!" yelled Samuel, waving his hands. He too, had caught a glimpse of her as she disappeared into the baggage collection area.

Hilde admired her two youngest children from a distance. She could hardly believe that her little Samuel was already a handsome schoolboy, and that Karoline, her little sweetie, had turned into a teenage beauty with long, shiny hair. She was shaken out of her reverie as both children sprinted off towards the arrivals area where Grandma Gjertrud had just come through the doors.

"Thank you so much for picking me up!" exclaimed Grandma Gjertrud, hugging and kissing everyone several times and trying not to topple over from receiving exuberant hugs from the two youngsters. Karoline and Samuel each grabbed one her suitcases and everyone headed to the car, chatting all the way.

"The weather's still good here, I see," said Grandma Gjertrud as they drove off. "No frost at night yet?"

"No," replied Hilde. "We've been lucky. The flowers are still blooming and the trees haven't yet started to lose their leaves. We have some apples still to harvest, but the weather is so beautiful that working in the garden is sheer pleasure these days."

Samuel was bouncing up and down in his seat, clearly bursting to say something. "Grandma Gjertrud, guess what?"

"What, honey?"

"Leela had three kittens a week ago and they have just opened their eyes!" he announced triumphantly, and then sat back proudly to watch Grandma Gjertrud's reaction.

"They are SO beautiful," Karoline added. "One of them is all yellow like his father and the other two are mixed colors, more like Leela."

"Oh, how wonderful!" Grandma Gjertrud said, smiling. "I'm looking forward to meeting them all, and I'm excited to hear how the two of you are doing at school. Tell me all about it!"

"I have already learned to write some letters," said Samuel. "My teacher is really nice. She reads aloud from a book while we eat our lunch and she knows a lot of funny stories, too."

"I'm glad to hear that," Grandma Gjertrud smiled at him.

"My school is okay," Karoline began speaking as they turned the car into their driveway.

"Tell me more about it when we get in, will you?" Grandma Gjertrud said as the car stopped in front of their house. "Don't forget to remind me."

After dinner Grandma Gjertrud disappeared into her room and returned with a bag full of presents." This is for the new schoolboy," she said, handing Samuel a nicely wrapped package. She realized he might not have the patience to wait for the others to unwrap their presents so she gave him his first. Samuel beamed and ripped off the paper impatiently.

"Wow..!" he murmured, as his eyes fell on a magnificent sword and shield made of soft grey foam.

"I have been in the land of the chevaliers, you see," Grandma Gjertrud said, happily smiling at Samuel's reaction. "So I was hoping that this might be just the right thing for my little chevalier at home."

"I love it!" he replied with shining eyes. "Just wait until my friend Rolf gets to see these. He'll be so impressed!" Samuel looked at his mum for approval and as soon as she nodded, he jumped up from his seat, grabbed his new weapon, and ran out the door to find his friend.

"This one is for you, honey," Grandma Gjertrud said, handing Karoline the next package. "I hope you will come to enjoy using it once you learn the basics."

"Thank you," Karoline said as she revealed a collection of six tubes of watercolor paint and a package of paint brushes in various shapes and sizes.

Grandma Gjertrud noticed that there was no smile on Karoline's face and no shine in her eyes as she looked at her present. She realized that there were now two topics they would need to look into by the end of the day. Karoline excused herself and withdrew to her room while the others received their gifts, one by one. Finally Grandma Gjertrud opened a bottle of rich, French red wine for the grownups to enjoy on such a lovely Saturday evening.

It was starting to get late when Grandma Gjertrud went to tuck Karoline in and have a chat. When she got to the room she was surprised to find the door was locked.

She hesitated, not sure what to do. Karoline was now a teenager, after all, and entitled to some privacy. The old lady took some time to look into herself for guidance and decided to reach out to Karoline. She knocked on the door and softly called out her name. "Karoline," she said. "Can I come in? I haven't said goodnight to you for such a long time and was hoping to have an evening chat with you, as well. Would that be alright?"

Karoline did not reply, but after awhile Grandma Gjertrud could hear her moving towards the door and a few seconds later, the door was unlocked and opened from the inside. As soon as Karoline saw Grandma Gjertrud, she looked down at her feet, turned around, and walked back to her bed. As she had left the door open, Grandma Gjertrud decided to follow her into the room. Karoline curled up under the bed-clothes, while Grandma Gjertrud sat down on a nearby chair.

"I'm sorry you didn't like the painting equipment, Karoline," she said. "I guess I got totally carried away with how much I was enjoying my painting course and I wanted to share that with you. It never occurred to me that you might not be interested. I'm sorry."

"It's not that I didn't like it. It is just that it made me feel like a total failure. I've never been any good at painting, plain and simple, and when you gave me those tubes of watercolor paint, it made me think of all the other things I don't seem to manage doing very well these days."

"Oh, honey," Grandma Gjertrud said, leaning forward and putting a hand carefully on Karoline's arm. "I've been away for so long. I have no idea what is going on in your life at the moment. Tell me all about your new school and how that's going."

Karoline pulled her legs tighter towards her chest and looked down at the quilt covering her bed. "They don't like me," she said, with sadness in her voice.

"They don't like you… " Grandma Gjertrud repeated, shaking her head in disbelief while waiting to see if Karoline would volunteer any more information.

"They don't like the way I do things anymore," Karoline went on.

"They don't like the way you do things anymore?" Grandma Gjertrud nodded and waited for her to respond.

"For instance, take my language teacher. I write my essays like I have always done, bending the topic just a little bit to give it an edge. Last year my language teacher loved it when I did that. This one seems to hate my style. She claims I'm using childish language and that I need to show some more feeling and reflection in the way I express my views, but I always feel a lot while writing, so why can't she see that in my essay? Is she dumb or something?"

Grandma Gjertrud had to think for a while before she felt prepared to comment on this outburst. Communicating with teachers was not one of her favorite things to do and she could very well understand how Karoline could feel misunderstood. Still she knew that going down that path would lead them both absolutely nowhere. She closed her eyes and started to breathe slowly and deeply, listening for guidance on how best to proceed.

"Are you telling me that you are doing things the way you used to do, while your teacher wants you to develop something that she thinks are more mature in style, and when she describes what she wants you to develop, she is unable to make you see her point?"

"Yes… something like that…" Karoline said. Although she kept her head bowed, Grandma Gjertrud could tell from the firmer tone in Karoline's voice that she was beginning to show an interest in the conversation.

"Okay, honey," Grandma Gjertrud said, looking straight at Karoline. "The problem here is just technique. That is something I can help you master. Being a year older means working a bit harder, that's all. Would you believe me if I said that this is not going to be your main problem this year?"

"Maybe…" Karoline sounded curious.

"Seems to me there is something else that is bothering you more." Grandma Gjertrud went still for a moment looking for guidance again. She felt like this conversation had been too superficial, that there was another layer to the story that had not yet been revealed. She took her time without getting impatient, stroking Karoline's hair while continuing to listen inwards waiting for the answer.

"Have you made new friends at school, honey?"

Karoline suddenly burst into tears, crying so hard that her whole body shook.

Grandma Gjertrud was a little taken aback. She felt like she had plucked the new topic totally out of the blue, but Karoline's reaction told her that she was on the right track.

"Well, yes... but then again, no..." Karoline sobbed.

"Are you saying you did make some new friends and now you have stopped being friends with them?"

"Something like that," Karoline replied.

"But, honey," Grandma Gjertrud was puzzled by now." What really happened? Do you not like them anymore?"

"Oh, yes!" Karoline said, her eyes lighting up.

"Then is there a particular reason why you are not friends with them anymore?"

Karoline started crying again as she struggled with her answer. "Well, Anne..."

"Anne is the reason you do not see your new friends any more, although you still like them. Did I get this right, honey?" Grandma Gjertrud felt a bit puzzled by the strange way this conversation was going.

"Yes," Karoline sniffed.

"I need you to fill me in on what has actually happened here. Would that be alright? I can see it makes you feel sad." Grandma Gjertrud knew she was onto something important, but she still felt confused. She looked at Karoline with great love and care, trying to send her courage to start talking about this confusing mess.

Karoline took a couple of deep breaths, found a more comfortable position on the bed, and started to explain.

"On my first day at the new school I noticed a small group of cool kids that caught my interest. I felt uncomfortable and shy, being new, but my curiosity won over my shyness and I went over and approached them. They turned out to be really friendly and before long I found myself invited to go bowling with them, trips to the movies, and Saturday evening gatherings. All the time I had this feeling of being appreciated and accepted. Soon I started to look forward to going to school and I felt happier than I have ever felt before. Then one afternoon Anne came to see me. She told me how disappointed she was that I didn't even talk to her during breaks at school, much less come to visit her. She cried and explained how dreadful and alone she had been feeling and that really made me feel ashamed. I have always considered myself a loyal and caring friend, and here was my best friend telling me that I was nothing but a self-centered snob. I could see that I was being a bit unfair, so I agreed to spend more time with her and less time with my new friends. That worked well for a while, but now she has asked me to choose between her and the others, and I have to give her an answer within a week." Karoline burst into tears again.

"Thank you for telling me about this, honey," Grandma Gjertrud said softly. "I understand this is really hard for you, and I am glad there is a whole week for you to find your answer. Now that I am back home I'll support you in any way you want me to, but right now you need to relax. How about we work on lifting your mood, and then I can show you a little trick I know to help you figure out what you really want. Does that sound good?" Grandma Gjertrud asked her with a smile on her face.

"Oh, that would be lovely," Karoline replied, sounding a bit brighter.

"Okay, honey. I will guide you through what I call the *Rolling Out Your Carpet* exercise. Lie down with your eyes closed and start, as usual, by thinking of something you love and expanding that feeling. Are you following me?"

"No problem so far," Karoline replied securely. This was something she knew well.

"Now take the question that you want help in finding an answer to, for example, what will you say to Anne by the end of the week. Imagine it as a Persian carpet, and then imagine the carpet rolling out in front of you. Picture sparkles of colored light raining down on the carpet as if the carpet was your little garden field and you were watering and fertilizing your plants. Keep going until the whole carpet or garden field feels saturated. Then ask that all the right circumstances, all the right people and all the right knowledge will come to you so that you can find a good answer, and then trust that they will. Remember to feel gratitude in your heart and imagine shouting, 'Thank you!' Add a few more golden sparkles for good measure and then roll the carpet back in. Now you can rest knowing that you've started working on the solution to your problem.

Okay?" Grandma Gjertrud looked at Karoline who nodded and took a deep breath.

"Good. Now roll over on your side and let me tuck you in."

Grandma Gjertrud started humming one of her old lullabies and Karoline was soon fast asleep.

Bedtime Story Number Nine

Paintbrushes and tubes of paint scattered on the carpet was the first thing that Karoline saw when she woke up. Her sleep had been deep and refreshing. No dreams or insights had been forthcoming though, and this fact disappointed her once she noticed it. So much for her hopes for a resolution to her dilemma with Anne using the exercise Grandma Gjertrud had taught her last night. "I should have realized this wouldn't work for me. Nothing works for me at the moment, that's for sure."

The more she thought about it, the worse it seemed. She climbed out of bed and kicked a couple of watercolor tubes over into the far corner of her room.

"Me? Painting? Never going to happen!" she sulked.

She put on her slippers and robe, and sneaked downstairs for some "Sunday-morning-alone-in-the-kitchen" food.

"Good morning, honey! How nice to see you!" Grandma Gjertrud called cheerily from the stove. The smell of bacon and eggs filled the kitchen. "Did you sleep well last night?"

Karoline stopped dead in her tracks. "Why are you up so early?" she said bluntly. "Did you forget it's Sunday?" As soon as the words were said, Karoline regretted them.

"I love you too!" Grandma Gjertrud replied calmly, her eyes warm and shiny.

Karoline hesitated. She had the feeling she knew an expression suitable for this occasion.

"Perfect timing," she said, laughing a bit.

"Oh, Karoline, I have missed you!" Grandma Gjertrud laughed too. "Come over here and give me a hug!"

Karoline hugged Grandma Gjertrud tightly and was surprised to feel tears welling in her eyes. "I have missed you, too, Grandma Gjertrud," she cried. "I just didn't realize it until now."

"Would you like to join me for some bacon and eggs?"

"I would love to! No one makes it as good as you. Have you made fried tomatoes with basil too?"

"Of course I have!" Grandma Gjertrud answered. "There are so many lovely tomatoes in the garden. Here, try one of these yellow ones!" She tossed over a small tomato and Karoline caught it in her mouth. They both laughed and sat down to breakfast.

"Right!" said Grandma Gjertrud, laying down her knife and fork with a satisfied air after finishing eating her meal. "Time to feed the animals. Can you give me a hand, Karoline?"

Karoline nodded and they headed outside, grabbing their farming coats and boots on the way. The morning air was crisp and clear and the light was beautiful. The sun had been up for a while already and they could feel it warming their faces." Look at all the apples lying on the ground," said Grandma Gjertrud. "I feel like making a big apple crumble this afternoon. Let's get the animals fed and we can gather the apples for it. It would be great to have some secret time together, too, if you would like that?" she said.

"Oh, I'd love to, Grandma Gertrud," Karoline responded.

The animals also seemed to be enjoying the autumn sunshine. The sheep crowded around the gate, eager for their food, and the chickens ran clucking into the yard as soon as the door to their pen was opened. When they were done feeding the animals, Grandma and Karoline spent half an hour or so picking up the fallen apples and putting them in crates.

"Karoline, could you bring me that basket over there?" Grandma said, standing up and stretching. "Goodness, my back hurts, but I don't want to waste these apples. Let's have a break and then we can gather up the rest and make them into applesauce later."

"Sure," said Karoline, picking up the basket. "Oh, Grandma Gjertrud!" she said, opening it. "You have brought tea and cookies for us. How sweet of you!"

"I have missed you. Remember that tea and cookies is one of our special things." Grandma poured the tea and sipped it as she warmed her face in the sun. "You should have seen the beautiful little town I stayed in, in France. The old part was actually a medieval castle surrounded by a huge ring of battlements with lots of towers. The only way in was across a bridge that was lowered over a moat, although nowadays it seems to be down all the time."

"That reminds me of the legend of Parzifal that you used to tell me when I was young," Karoline said, remembering the old story. "Did you not promise me that you would tell me more about how to find my Inner Voice?"

"Perfect timing," Grandma Gjertrud said, smiling. "I'm so glad you remembered that! When you think about it, you and Parzifal actually have a lot in common. You are both young and in search of your own personality and the purpose of your life. You are unsure about how to behave, whose advice to trust, and who not to listen to. Learning to make your own decisions can make you vulnerable."

"And we are both struggling to develop and trust our Inner Voice," Karoline added.

"Exactly."

"Grandma Gjertrud, I am sorry for being so hostile toward you this morning."

"That's okay, honey. Have you any idea why you were irritated?"

Karoline nodded. "I was disappointed that the Peace Exercise you taught me last night didn't give me any information or help during my sleep," she said.

"I can see how that could make you feel bad. Would you like to work on that?"

"Um, yes..." Karoline said, surprised that Grandma Gjertrud was not going to defend herself.

"Okay." Grandma Gjertrud sat up straight. "Can I ask you to walk in a circle in front of me?"

Karoline started walking.

"Now show me with your body and the way you move how it feels to be disappointed like you were this morning. Show me how it feels when I say these sentences: 'Grandma Gjertrud's *Rolling Out Your Carpet* exercise did not help me at all. Grandma Gjertrud does not know how to help me. Nobody knows how to help me. I am never going to learn the things my teacher's demand of me. I am never going to learn how to paint.' " Grandma Gjertrud watched Karoline as she walked slower and slower.

"This is great Karoline!" Grandma Gjertrud said. "You are bending your head, letting your back fall forward, arms just hanging down, and your steps are slow and plodding. Do you like this feeling?"

"NO!" Karoline answered firmly.

"Good! Now deliberately change the way you walk. Straighten up your back, hold your head up, square off your shoulders, and start to walk faster, using the soles of your feet actively to move more efficiently. Do you like *this* feeling?"

"Yes!" said Karoline, starting to smile.

"Right. Keep up the speed while I ask you some more questions. Are you ready?"

"I am," Karoline answered. She was beginning to have problems talking normally, given how fast she was walking.

"Good. Now shout out the answers to the following questions without hesitation, preferably without thinking about your responses. Remember, you can always change your mind later if you feel like it. Right now we are just looking for your spontaneous replies, okay?"

"Okay!"

"The *Roll Out Your Carpet Exercise* might be able to help me find my Inner Voice. True or false?"

"True!"

"There are people who know how to help me. True or false?"

"True!"

"I can learn how to give my teachers what they want without losing myself in the process. True or false?"

"True!"

"I can learn how to paint if I decide to. True or false?"

"True!" Karoline's eyes started shining brighter as she gave the answers.

"I am tired of this exercise and want to stop now. True or false?"

"True!" Karoline gasped, collapsing in a fit of giggles. Grandma Gjertrud laughed too. She was quite happy with how things were going.

"You did very well, Karoline," Grandma Gjertrud said. "Did you like it?"

"Oh yes!"

"Describe to me what you feel you have learned from this new exercise."

"Well…" Karoline had to think it over a bit before she could reply. "When I was sad and tried to express that while walking, I felt even sadder, but when I deliberately straightened my body and started walking faster, I soon felt better."

"Did you have to feel better to be able to walk straight?" Grandma Gjertrud asked, trying to drive home the lesson.

"No. As soon as I decided to straighten up, I felt better."

"Perfect, honey. You are doing so well! You should be really proud of yourself, you know. Learning to take responsibility for your feelings is very important." Grandma Gjertrud said. "Do you think that you can manage to work a little bit more on this?"

"Yes!" Karoline replied quickly. She had not felt this good for weeks and didn't want to quit just yet.

"Good. Do you remember the Root Exercise I taught you when you were a little girl?"

"You bet!" Karoline immediately started to bounce up and down, bending her knees and taking a couple of deep breaths. She then stopped and imagined growing a root from the lowest point of her spine, letting it work its way deep into the ground. After having sent all her frustrations and worries down the root she let the comforting, soothing, strengthening power from deep inside the Earth enter her body through the stalk.

"Good work, Karoline. Now straighten your back and keep your head held high. Imagine your spine extending upwards as a cord, growing out through the top of your head and up into the sky, all the way up to the stars and galaxies. Let the power from up there flow down the cord and into your spine. Feel how that lightens up your whole body. You are doing fine, Karoline. Can you feel how this part of the exercise makes it easier to keep your body straight?"

"Yes," Karoline said. She was surprised. "It feels like the cord is helping me to keep my head up. Is that really so?"

"You are so right, honey!" Grandma Gjertrud assured her. She smiled to herself. It was good to see how Karoline had changed from being a suspicious and lost girl to an excited and confident one in such a short while. She realized the job was far from done, but it sure was a promising start.

Bedtime Story Number Ten

Karoline was exhausted and irritable when she came home from school the next afternoon. She had been so busy all day she had not even had a chance to eat her lunch.

"I'm starving!" she complained as she threw her school bag on the floor and flopped down on the nearest chair.

"Oh honey, did you forget to take your lunch box today?" Grandma Gjertrud asked, giving Karoline a hug and picking up her school bag.

"No, I just didn't have time to eat. There were things happening all the time and during our main break, Anne wanted to talk to me. So we went outside to get some privacy and I forgot to bring my food. While an omelet with vegetables is my favorite dish, you must admit it is not the kind of food you can nibble on from under your desk during classes. And my language teacher had to pick on me, just to make my day even worse."

"How about you sit down and eat your lunch now, honey?" Grandma Gjertrud suggested.

"The last thing I feel like doing is eating!" said Karoline crossly.

Grandma Gjertrud could tell Karoline was irritated, but she couldn't figure out how much was due to the fact that Karoline had not eaten and how much came from her having had some bad experiences at school. She quickly decided to address both problems at the same time. She knew that being hungry could lower a person's tolerance for all kinds of things and make everything seem a lot worse. She also knew that it takes the body quite a while to process a whole meal into useable energy.

"Let's both have a glass of the apple juice I made this morning," she suggested, putting two glasses and a bottle of juice on the table. *Time to set a good example,* she thought.

"I think this is the best juice I have ever made. Don't you agree?" Grandma Gjertrud finished pouring the juice and started to drink some. After a moment, Karoline picked up her glass and took a sip, then quickly emptied the glass.

"Give the juice five or ten minutes to get into your system and you should start to feel better. If you want, you can lie down on the kitchen couch and relax. I will put on some music for you to enjoy while you're waiting." Grandma Gjertrud put on one of her favorite Mozart CDs and left the room.

Some minutes later she returned with a bucket full of freshly harvested vegetables.

"Now, how about you eat your omelet and keep me company while I start dinner?" she smiled, passing Karoline her lunch box. The blood sugar issue might be resolved, but Grandma could sense that Karoline wasn't happy.

School must be very demanding these days, when the pupils are so frustrated on the first day of the week, Grandma Gjertrud thought to herself. *What do these teachers think they're doing? All they seem to do is cram the children's heads with facts and then pick on them when they do things wrong. How are we ever going to create peace in the world if things continue on like this? They need to think about what they're passing on to these vulnerable young people. They should encourage them to be themselves, help them experience mastering, and celebrate their successes instead of teaching them to trample everyone else in pursuit of their goals.*

Grandma Gjertrud realized her thoughts were leading her in the wrong direction. She did not want to join the choir of complainers in the world, so she quickly rearranged them. She took a moment to think about something she really loved and as soon as she felt her mood picking up, she turned her focus back to Karoline. She realized that she would have to be the teacher, filling in where the others had failed, and help secure Karoline a better life in the future.

"What are we having for dinner?" Karoline asked. Her blood sugar and energy levels were back to normal, so she was now able to notice things going on around her. Now she could see Grandma Gjertrud had finished washing and peeling the vegetables.

"To be honest, I don't have a clue," Grandma Gjertrud answered. "Normally when I make food, I start by deciding what I want to make and seeing whether I have roughly the right ingredients, but from there I tend to manage the details mostly by inspiration. Today, though, my mind is blank. Do you have any suggestions?

"I think you should make a casserole," said Karoline at once. "Yours always taste good, and they can look after themselves once they are in the oven. Maybe you and I could have some time to chat."

"Perfect suggestion," Grandma Gjertrud replied. "I won't even fry the meat all the way through. I'll just cut it into smaller pieces and start cooking it in some apple juice and wine as the meat needs takes longer to cook than the rest of the ingredients. If you'll help me cut the vegetables they will be ready to put in the pot after the meat has cooked for a while. Then all we need to do is add some herbs, salt, and spices to finish it all up. Why don't you tell me how school was today while we do the chopping?"

"I don't think that I am ready to talk about all the Anne stuff yet, but I would love to tell you how badly my language teacher treated me today," Karoline said, sounding quite frustrated. "Do you know what that idiot did? He was handing back the book reviews we passed in last week and when he came to my review, he looked at me and said, 'This was not good enough, Karoline. Please give me a proper one by the end of the week!' As if my pile of homework isn't big enough without him making me do it twice!" Karoline's voice was angry, but Grandma Gjertrud could tell how hurt she was under the anger.

"He doesn't like me, that's obvious. I have tried to write what I think about that book, but he doesn't like my opinion, so what more can I do? He is not going to be satisfied with me no matter what I hand in at the end of the week. I might as well give up!" Karoline had stopped cutting vegetables and was waving her knife in the air to emphasize her words.

"Can I read your book review, Karoline?" Grandma Gjertrud asked. "It might help if I understand why you feel the way you do."

Karoline pulled the book review out of her bag and handed it over to Grandma Gjertrud. It did not take an old teacher like Grandma Gjertrud long to discover what might be the problem.

"I think I understand why you and your teacher don't seem to understand each other," Grandma Gjertrud said." Would you like me to try to explain it to you?"

"Any time," Karoline answered, although Grandma Gjertrud was far from convinced she truly wanted to hear what she had to say.

"I know you have always loved to do things your own way, or by 'bending the rules' as you usually put it,"

Grandma Gjertrud started to explain. "I remember once when your old language teacher asked you to write an interview, you insisted on interviewing a little child that could hardly speak. Because you are such a good writer, your text and the way you used the language was excellent, so your teacher chose to give you good marks, even though you did not actually do what he had asked you to do. You see, when he asked you to write an interview, he was expecting you first to study the formula on how to conduct an interview, and then make an interview where you showed him you were familiar with the method and knew how to use it. This applies to writing a book review as well. I think that all you need is to learn the method for writing a book review, then, in time and with experience, you can apply your tendency to bend the rules and still have a solid book review at the end of the process."

"Think back to how we made the casserole just now. I could improvise because I've been making casseroles for years. Yet if I didn't know how to make a casserole, it's best to start by following a recipe. Once I've done that a couple of times and am familiar with the ingredients and methods, I can start to play around a bit and improvise, and still be pretty sure that the casserole will turn out well. If I was to improvise first without knowing the recipe, chances are it would be a disaster."

"But I don't have the method for writing a book review," Karoline complained.

"Well, honey, that we will give you right here and now. Ready?"

"Oh, just give it to me!" Karoline said, starting to look happier.

"Okay. This recipe contains seven 'ingredients' or points and normally you need to include them all." Grandma Gjertrud started to make points on a page in her notebook.

"Point 1 – All the facts: title, writer's name, number of pages in the book, name of publisher and year of publishing."

"Point 2 – Other titles by the same author."

"Point 3 – A short description of what is happening in the book. Make sure not to reveal the outcome.

"Point 4 – What kind of literary figures of speech the author has used. Here you need to make sure to use examples from the text, preferably for more than one of the devices. Possible devices would be: repetition, similes, metaphors, foreshadowing, etc."

"Point 5 – What you thought of the book; your opinion goes in here. Use examples and make sure to explain why you react or think the way you do."

"Point 6 – Who should read this book? How old would they be?"

"Point 7 – Choose a title for your review and try to let the title express what you feel about the book."

"That's it! Make sure to follow these points and anybody will know it's is a proper book review, honey! Let's go back and look at the review you have already written. Can you see anything in your review that is not following this method?"

Karoline looked at her text for a while and compared it to the steps on Grandma Gjertrud's notepad. Suddenly her eyes lit up as she said, "I seem to have mixed my own opinion and the neutral description in the same part of the text. Is that what you mean?"

"Quite right. Now if you divide that text and put the descriptive words in the part where they belong and your opinions in the section for your opinion, you will probably find that in both places there will be something missing. But this will be easier to fill in as you now know what kind of information belongs where. Do you agree?"

"Absolutely," Karoline said. She was beginning to believe she would be able to make this book review work and that made her feel happy and relieved. "But now I can see that there is actually one part of the process that is not there at all, the part where I describe what kind of literary figures of speech the author has used. I could really use some advice on that one. Will you help me, Grandma Gjertrud?"

Grandma Gjertrud was happy to help, and when they were done, Karoline sat down at her computer, moved parts of her old text to the right places and added what was needed to make her book review meet the standard method for book reviews.

"But why on earth didn't the teacher explain it to me right away, just like you did?" Karoline was starting to get quite angry. "It would have saved me a lot of trouble!"

"I would rather not comment on that question." Grandma Gjertrud sighed. "I'll just pay forward what we have always said in my family which is 'Better use your head if you've got one.' This means you should go ahead and sort out your problems if you can rather than waiting for others to take the initiative, because chances are they never will."

After dinner that night before anyone had left the table, Grandma Gjertrud tapped on her glass and rose to give a little speech. "Dear friends," she said. "I believe it is important to celebrate whatever successes we have, and make sure we focus on what we want more of in life. I would like to celebrate a little miracle that has taken place in our house today. You may have noticed that Karoline has had some problems communicating with her teachers lately. Part of being a teenager is about getting to know yourself and finding your own way around the obstacles in life. But to be able to find out who you really are, you also have to be willing to try things you have never done before. Today Karoline tried her best to understand the reason why one of her teacher's grading practices bothered her. In this process she not only managed to find out why the two of them had problems understanding each other, she also made the necessary changes on her book review so that her teacher will realize that Karoline has grown in her understanding of the subject. For all this excellent work, Karoline, I honor you and ask all of you to join me in making a toast to Karoline's new achievements." Everyone at the table raised their glasses.

When Karoline entered her room to go to bed that evening, she suddenly decided to pick up the six tubes of paint and all the brushes that had been lying on her carpet for days. She was carefully putting them on her desk as Grandma Gjertrud knocked on the door.

"I just wanted to give you this little book," Grandma Gjertrud said and handed her a beautiful small notebook covered in purple satin. "I challenge you to write at least three sentences in this book every evening, ones where you celebrate what you are proud of having achieved that day, and you must never mention the same thing twice. This will help you focus on your successes, not your problems, and by keeping such a focus, you will get more of what you want."

Karoline gave Grandma Gjertrud a big, heartfelt hug and ran her fingers slowly and lovingly over the satin cover.

Bedtime Story Number Eleven

"I think I want to start watercolor painting today. Will you show me how to do it?" Karoline asked Grandma Gjertrud at breakfast.

"I would love to, honey," Grandma Gjertrud answered. She was delighted to see that Karoline was starting to take more charge of her own life. "When do you want to start?"

"Could we begin this afternoon? I have to make dinner, but I've got most of my homework for the week finished and I get home early today."

"Seems like perfect timing to me," Grandma smiled.

Karoline's dad laid down the newspaper he was reading. "I'm working from home today," he said, "So I'd be happy to make the dinner for you if you like." He realized that this was a real breakthrough for his daughter and wanted to support her in any way he could.

"Why don't you use my lecture room in the new barn?" Hilde added. "It'll save you the hassle of being disturbed by the boys when they get home."

"Oh, that's awesome!" Karoline blurted out, smiling from ear to ear. "I can't wait to get home from school today!"

"Here is your lunch box," Grandma Gjertrud said, handing it to Karoline. "Bacon omelet today."

"Perfect!" Karoline said. "And I promise you I'll eat it on my lunch break this time!" She gave Grandma Gjertrud a big hug before running out the door.

"I don't know what you've done to Karoline since you got back from France, Grandma Gjertrud, but whatever it is, I want you to know that Hilde and I are very grateful," said Henrik. He and Grandma Gjertrud were sitting in the kitchen enjoying an extra cup of tea after the rest of the family had left the house. "We've watched her get more and more introverted since she started this new school, and seeing her smile again this morning really made my heart sing!"

"She is a treasure, that girl. What more can I say?" Grandma Gjertrud replied.

Henrik studied his hands for a moment and then went on. "Actually, I'm very grateful for all you've done for my family. Since we bought the farm and moved in here with you so many things have changed for the better in our lives. But what about you, Grandma Gjertrud? Are you happy? Are we doing enough to help *you* thrive?" Henrik had grown very fond of Grandma Gjertrud. He would have loved to give her a hug, but he was a reserved man who hadn't been brought up to give spontaneous hugs and he felt rather awkward about it so he did nothing.

"Oh, Henrik, thank you so much for asking," Grandma Gjertrud replied. "But I can assure you my life has become so much more meaningful since you and your family joined me. It's such a joy to have the children around, and such a comfort to know that you and Hilde are here in the house with me. And the painting seminar in France that you gave me for my birthday this year was so amazingly good, I will never forget it."

Grandma Gjertrud seemed to glow as she spoke. Henrik could sense how happy and grateful she was and the warmth in his heart seemed to bubble over. Without giving himself time to change his mind, he got up and gave her a big hug. Grandma Gjertrud was surprised. She knew how unlike Henrik this was, and realized how hard it must have been for him to do that. She showed her appreciation by hugging him back warmly. "You are a great man, Henrik," she said. "I admire your strength and knowledge, but most of all I love your spiritual intuition. Thank you for that lovely hug!"

When Karoline got home from school, she found Grandma Gjertrud already painting in the lecture room.

"Good to see you, honey. How was your day at school?"

"Fine," said Karoline. "You should have seen my language teacher's expression when I handed him my book review! He was quite suspicious, but at least he gave me some credit for it, which is cool. And by the way, I did remember to eat," Karoline grinned.

Grandma Gjertrud chuckled. "Did you even remember to bring your painting equipment with you just now?" she asked.

"Yes, I did," Karoline said, proud to have remembered. "Strangely enough I have already started to like the paints and brushes. It's like we belong together." She put down her bag and took everything out of it. There were two shades of red paint, two of yellow, and two of blue.

"Right then!" Grandma Gjertud exclaimed. "I suggest we start off with a painting exercise that I learned from my first painting teacher many years ago. I still use it when I haven't been painting for a while and want to start again. You will need a wet piece of watercolor paper, the red, yellow, and blue paint, and a quite a big brush."

Grandma Gjertrud showed Karoline how to soak her paper in a basin of clean water for a few minutes and then smooth it carefully onto the table. Then she helped her put a little bit of each color of paint, well apart, around the edges of a plate. She showed her how to first dip the brush in water, then in blue paint, and then mix the water and paint together a bit by turning the brush around on a clear spot of the plate a couple of times. She explained that they would start painting from the left corner of the paper across to the right in a horizontal manner.

"First you breathe in deeply," grandma Gjertrud said. "Then you put down the brush and draw it slowly and steadily toward the right side of the page while breathing out slowly."

Karoline put down her brush and while breathing out she painted a thick, deep blue line along the bottom of the paper.

"It almost feels like I am breathing out that line of color," Karoline said. "How cool!"

Grandma Gjertrud next showed her how to dip the brush in water, collect more blue color while breathing in, and then exhaling while painting a new, blue line right above the former one, leaving no part of the paper showing between the lines. They carried on like this until the first third of the paper was all blue, and then washed the brush and switched to yellow for the next third, before switching to red.

"You can do this exercise whenever you feel like painting, but don't know what you want to paint," Grandma Gjertrud explained. "It is actually a nice way of relaxing. If you want to, you can use all six colors and give them one sixth of the paper each, or you can let the colors blend slowly into each other and see what effect that has. You can even dilute each color with more and more water, making it fade out before you bring in the next color. Remember that you can always remove most of a color even after you have painted it, by simply rinsing the brush in water and then repainting the area using only clean water. This applies to painting on wetted paper which is what I recommend you do in the beginning."

Karoline finished her exercise in silence with a big smile and sparkling eyes.

"Seems to me you are having a good time, Karoline," said Grandma.

"Much to my surprise, I am," Karoline replied. "I have never been good at drawing, but this is something totally different. I feel like the brush is an extension of my hand."

"I know exactly what you mean, honey," Grandma Gjertrud said. "That makes two of us."

They painted for a while. Karoline continued with breathing the colors, but Grandma Gjertrud worked on a painting of a body with rainbow-like color combinations radiating from it. When they got tired, they took a break, enjoying some herbal tea, some cookies, and a chat, and then they returned to their painting. They did not talk much; they were happily absorbed in playing with the colors. When Karoline had tried using all six colors, she asked Grandma Gjertrud for more guidance. Grandma suggested they start to think of water, lakes, rivers, oceans, waves, big waves, and storms.

"Try moving as if you were water; floating, running wild, being caught by the wind and thrown ahead or whatever else you can imagine would happen to you if you were a body of water," Grandma Gjertrud suggested.

Karoline moved. She had always liked dancing and found this to be a fun challenge.

"Now stop moving and start painting the movement instead. Paint how it is to be water," Grandma Gjertrud said.

"How do I do that?" Karoline suddenly felt herself become all stiff and uncertain again. She had no idea how to paint water and was afraid she'd get it wrong.

"You take some blue color on your brush and continue the arm movements that you made when you were being water. Remember this is for fun! Just play with it and see how you feel. If you don't like it, at least you will know that and you can always try again some other day," Grandma Gjertrud encouraged her. "Remember that water usually contains many shades of blue, which means you get to mix your brush with more or less water. You can also use both the blue colors in different amounts; that will give you different shades of blue. You might even try mixing in a little bit of one of the red colors to get some darker parts in the blue."

Karoline gave it a try and soon got hooked on the blue water movements, experimenting with Grandma's suggestions. She had a lovely time. When she was done with water, she did the same with trees. She imagined being a tree, moving like a tree, and Grandma Gjertrud showed her how to mix blue and yellow together to make green so that she could paint how it felt to be a tree.

"How many colors is it possible to make?" Karoline asked when she started to get tired.

"There are three basic colors – blue, red, and yellow," Grandma Gjertrud replied, as she started to tidy up. "The reason I gave you two of each is that they are a little bit different in quality and will give different impressions when you mix them. One type has a warm quality to it while the other type is colder. When you mix both together, you get the 'true' color. Some people say that the colors in the rainbow are all the colors we have, but as you have seen this afternoon, the possibilities for mixing colors seems to be infinite," she smiled. They finished cleaning their brushes and went back to the house for dinner.

After dinner Karoline asked if she could go and paint some more. Grandma Gjertrud noticed her eagerness with great satisfaction and chose to stay at the dinner table a bit longer to give her some time to experiment on her own. In the meantime she poured herself a glass of red wine and settled back to enjoy watching Karoline's growing enthusiasm for painting.

Karoline looked up with an excited smile as Grandma Gjertrud joined her in the lecture room. "Come here! Look at what I made while you were finishing dinner!"

"Wow, this is fantastic, Karoline!" Grandma Gjertrud burst out. "You have made a rainbow! How impressive. With all the right colors following on top of each other. Red, orange, yellow, green, blue, indigo and violet. Good work!"

"I saw the rainbow you were working on and wanted to try something similar," Karoline explained.

"Oh, you mean the aura I am struggling with?" Grandma Gjertrud asked.

"Or-a what?" Karoline said. She had obviously never heard the word before.

"An aura," Grandma Gjertrud started to explain. "It is a field of vibration or radiation surrounding a living being. I must admit that not all people believe in the existence of auras, but let's play with the thought that it is really there. It is said that all that happens to you in your lifetime will be stored as vibrational information in your aura, meaning that those who can see such things can tell a lot about you by looking at it.

"Can you see auras, Grandma Gjertrud?" Karoline asked curiously.

"No, I don't perceive things as light or color," Grandma Gjertrud said. "I tend to sense the vibration field, or aura, with my palms if I very slowly approach a person. So in my painting, I was just playing with what I think an aura would look like. You already noticed that I used the rainbow colors and I like to look at it the way it is now. Speaking of rainbow colors, let me show you this painting that I made in France." Grandma Gjertrud opened her portfolio of paintings and picked one out. She had drawn the outline of a person and then painted what looked like seven flowers along the person's spine from bottom to top. The flowers were painted in the colors of the rainbow, starting off with red at the bottom and ending with pale violet floating above the head.

"These flowers are beautiful, Grandma Gjertrud," Karoline said. "Do they mean anything special or did you just invent them?"

"That is a well put question," Grandma Gjertrud answered. "I was trying to paint something called 'chakras.' Chakras are said to be vibrational centers seated along our spine. The use of colors has to do with the vibrational qualities believed to belong to the different chakras. The lowest one, called the Root Chakra, has the deepest or slowest vibration, just like the color red has the slowest vibration of the seven rainbow colors. The next chakra is the Hara Chakra, and its orange color indicates that it has a higher vibration than the former one. As you move further up through the other chakras, the vibration speeds up according to the colors I have painted, all the way to the top where the violet color is indicating the highest frequency or vibration."

"Are you telling me that the highest seated of the seven chakras, the one on top of the head, is actually the strongest one since it has the highest vibrational rate?" Karoline asked.

"No, not really," Grandma Gjertrud answered. "High vibration does not necessarily mean intense or strong vibration. Let me try to make this a bit clearer for you. A vibration can be a color, a sound, or just a radiation of energy. Each color, sound, or radiation energy has their own individual vibrational frequency, making it possible to separate it from something similar. If you want to paint using one of your red colors, you would put some of it on a plate, dip your brush in water then in the red paint, and touch the paper. If you used a lot of color, the color red would look very intense, and if you used a little color diluting it with more water, the red would pale, but they would all be versions of the same vibrational red color. It's the same with our chakras. Their vibration will fit one of the colors of the rainbow, but the intensity of it may vary throughout our life depending on various things. This means that some of your chakras may vibrate strongly, transmit a lot of color, while other chakras may be weak transmitting less color. This can be a reason why people's auras can be dominated by some of the rainbow colors, showing little or nothing of the other ones."

"The use of chakras is a very old practice in Eastern religions like Buddhism and Hinduism. They often describe more chakras than these and each chakra might have flowers where each petal has different colors. The way I have painted it belongs to a more modern interpretation, made by people who believe that even old traditions might benefit from renewal as we are always moving forward toward new challenges. There are so many more interesting things I can tell you about both auras and chakras, but that will have to wait until some other time. My reason for mentioning it today was to show you the similarities in the use of colors in these systems, based on the vibrational qualities of each color."

Grandma Gjertrud suddenly stopped talking, as she realized it was really late and Karoline should have been in bed already.

"We will have to wrap up now, honey," she said. "Thank you for joining me today, Karoline. It made me want to come here more often to paint."

"Me, too," Karoline said, hugging Grandma Gjertrud warmly.

Bedtime Story Number Twelve

Karoline skipped up the driveway. She'd been listening to the church bells ringing all the way home from school and that always cheered her up. She was pleasantly surprised to find Uncle Bernt and Samuel playing outside as she approached the house.

"Uncle Bernt!" she called out. She threw off her schoolbag and ran to greet him with a big hug. "I had no idea you would be coming today!"

"Nor did I," Uncle Bernt replied, receiving her hug with a big smile. "Something reminded me that I had not seen you guys for quite a while, so here I am. Would you like to join Samuel and me in these experiments?"

Karoline was taken by surprise and did not know what to say. She was not used to playing with a seven year old, but joining Uncle Bernt in an experiment sounded like something she would consider. "Sure," she replied after a moment or two. "What are you guys doing?"

"We are throwing stones into the ducks big bathtub and watching how they make circles in the water!" Samuel replied excitedly. "Watch this one!" He threw a medium-size stone into the tub. The water immediately reacted, forming circles that radiated out towards the wall of the tub.

"Let's try something new," Uncle Bernt suggested. "If each of you finds a stone and throws it into the water at the same time, we can see what happens as the circles from the two stones meet. Are you in?"

Both Samuel and Karoline were already hunting for stones. "Right. Both throw your stones in on the count of three," Uncle Bernt said, and immediately started counting. On three, Karoline and Samuel threw their stones into the water. Both stones made circles, but as the circles met, one circle seemed to overtake the other.

"My circle was stronger than yours," Samuel said with a confident smile.

"Mine will be stronger next time," Karoline replied. It seemed reasonable that since she was much older than her brother, she should be able to throw a stone and make circles strong enough to conquer his. She was already looking for a new stone, as was Samuel.

"Ready? Again on three?" Uncle Bernt said.

They both threw their stones, but Karoline was surprised to discover the circles of her stone were invaded even further by Samuel's this time.

"Yes!" Samuel shouted, running around with his hands in the air like a champion.

"As if I cared," Karoline said sulkily. Mostly to herself, she added sadly, "This seems to be the story of my life; everybody invading my space..."

"Come here, honey," Uncle Bernt whispered. He had heard her comment and immediately knew why he was supposed to be here today. "Will you let me give you some advice?" he asked.

Karoline was disappointed and cross, and the last thing she wanted was advice, but as this was Uncle Bernt, she felt she could not say no. "Bring it on," she replied a little sarcastically.

"Your brother has already noticed that he can affect the intensity of the waves by putting more force or speed into his arm while throwing the stone," Uncle Bernt whispered. "How about you have another go, without you telling Samuel that you know his secret?"

Karoline nodded ever so slightly, and smiling to herself a little she picked up a third stone, a little larger than the last one. "Hey Samuel!" she shouted. "Want to try one last time?"

Samuel ran over to the tub, grabbed the nearest stone, and was ready to conquer his sister once more. They tossed in their stones, but this time the circles from Karoline's stone's ripple went right through those from Samuel's rock. Samuel stood and looked in surprise at the water as Karoline burst into joyous laughter. She felt like there was a little sun exploding inside her filling her with light and warmth.

"Seems like your sister has discovered how to do it as well," Uncle Bernt said to Samuel, winking at him. They both laughed. Just then Samuel's friend Rolf came up the path to see what was going on. Samuel enthusiastically told him all about it, and soon the two boys were totally focused on stones and water circles, oblivious of anything else going on around them.

"Let's go inside to tell Grandma Gjertrud," Uncle Bernt suggested to Karoline. Karoline nodded and hurried to pick up her schoolbag, eager to tell Grandma Gjertrud all about what she'd learned about throwing rocks into water.

After dinner all three children stayed at the kitchen table watching Uncle Bernt enjoying his favorite cup of special, herbal coffee, knowing he would answer their questions and tell more stories once he had finished.

"Okay, Olaf, would you like to ask the first question today?" Uncle Bernt said, looking Olaf squarely in the face.

"I'm starting to get confused, Uncle Bernt," Olaf said. "All these things that you have been telling us over the years, they have been so exciting and fascinating, but when I try to talk to other people about them, they seem to think it is all just fantasy and imagination. Even my science teachers tell me to stop believing things that have long been proven wrong. Why are you still telling us these things if they are just fantasy, Uncle Bernt?" Olaf sounded frustrated.

"Well, that is the best question I have heard for ages!" Uncle Bernt replied. "You are summing up some real big problems going on in the world! People have so many different theories and opinions about the world and how it works, and some of them are very different from others. I think everyone is partially right. The important thing is to realize that how we see life is based on our experience and our beliefs. We take what we already know and use that to make assumptions about things we don't know about yet, including things that no one really knows about, like how the world started and how the universe works. We use the things that we already know to fill in the blanks. Let me give you an analogy to make this a bit clearer. Picture all of creation as being a giraffe, rubbing itself against a large building with many windows. There's a person looking out of each window, but each person is only able to see one little piece of the giraffe, the section that is showing outside their window. Let's say these people can all communicate easily with each other and they agree to find out what it is that's outside the building. A person looking out of a high window will see the top of the giraffe's head and claim that the creature has two ossicones or what some people call horns. A person on the ground floor will see four legs and say the creature is long and thin with brown spots. Someone in the middle will agree that the creature has brown spots, but say that it is a huge creature that fills the world outside. The person at the top will only see blue sky above its head. What do you think he would report back to the others?"

"He would have to claim there was no such thing as the creature, wouldn't he?" Olaf said, trying to figure out how this applied to real life.

"That's right, Olaf," Uncle Bernt replied. "The thing is, each person is correct. They all sincerely report what they see and stand up for what they understand to be the truth, but each version is very different from the others. Imagine the arguments that could break out! And all because no one has realized that they're all looking at different parts of the same animal! For a long time, our society has believed that scientists are the only ones standing outside the building and able to see the whole giraffe. If this was the case, then of course their description would be the only accurate one, and the descriptions given by people inside the building who can only seeing out one window, must be flawed and could safely be discounted as the truth. But what if the scientists are really inside the building, too, and just don't realize it? What if no one, in fact, has the whole picture? In that case, everyone is partially right, but everyone is also partially wrong. Do you see how this applies to our world, Olaf?"

"Yes, I think so... " Olaf said slowly. "You mean that different ways of explaining the world, like science, different religions, or the exciting things you've told us about... they're all views from different windows; all parts of reality, but none of them is the whole thing?"

"Exactly!" Uncle Bernt replied. "Realizing this makes it easier for me to be humble and respectful towards people whose opinions are very different to mine."

"Still, I get confused having all these different versions inside my head and trying to figure out if what I believe is true or not." Olaf said.

"I know, Olaf," Uncle Bernt said, nodding. "How about you try a technique I learned when I was young? They say it was invented by the great Napoleon Bonaparte, and you'll agree he had a lot to think about, what with creating an empire! What he did was to imagine a problem being like a chest of drawers. When he was thinking about, say which country to invade next, he would imagine pulling out the drawer which contained all the necessary information he needed to know so he could work on creating a plan of attack. When it was time to think about what to have for lunch, he would close the 'countries to invade' drawer, and then open the 'what to eat' drawer. Of course, I'm being silly, but the point is he could think about one set of things at a time without everything getting confused."

"Are you suggesting I should make a drawer for all of your stories, Uncle Bernt?" Olaf said.

"Well, you might even consider making more than one drawer. My point is that whenever you are confronted with a statement or theory that you think sounds incredible, impossible, or unbelievable, you can put it in a drawer and shut that drawer if you want, not having to think about it in your daily life. If something happens, though, and you get some more strange information, you might open that drawer again to see if there is something in there that matches the information you just received. Pairing different pieces of information over the years might give you some new ways of looking at things, and it's never wrong to be open for new solutions. How else is peace going to have a chance in this world which is full of disagreements?"

"Can I ask a question now?" Karoline said. She had been listening to Uncle Bernt's explanation with some impatience. Although the topic was exciting, and she felt that inventing a drawer for strange information would definitely be a thing she would like to try, there was something else more important to her right now. "Can you tell me some more about water and water circles, like the ones we just made outside . . . and vibration? Some people say that water has a memory of its own. Is that true?"

"Wow, you guys are asking me some great questions today," Uncle Bernt said. He looked at Karoline, pretending not to notice Samuel sneaking away from the table on his way out. Samuel was bored by Uncle Bernt's explanations and Karoline's question had reminded him that he'd much rather be playing with rocks and the water.

"Water is an exciting element," Uncle Bernt began. "All life is totally dependent on it. Your body, for instance, contains about sixty percent water. That means you are actually carrying between two and three buckets of water inside your body all the time. It's actually amazing that you can't hear it slosh inside you as you move!" Karoline grinned and Uncle Bernt went on. "As with all other substances, the molecules that make up water are vibrating all the time. As you could see from our experiment outside, water adjusts more easily than most things to what's happening in its surroundings. We can see that it boils if it gets hot enough, and freezes if it gets cold enough. It will move if it is hit by something, and fall down if it runs over a cliff. It can even transport electricity. The way the molecules vibrate might even change, taking on the vibration of their surroundings, and some people call this *memory*, meaning that the vibration of the water will reflect what has happened to it. Other people claim they can consciously send their thoughts or prayers into water, believing that water will then have a better vibration than it had before. In our society, this idea can be found in the use of Holy Water in Christian churches, but other cultures also have such beliefs. Some cultures believe you need to cleanse your body using specially prepared water, both externally and internally, as part of the preparation for initiation or enlightenment.

"Most people agree that it's important to drink lots of water, since our kidneys need it to filter undesirable substances out of our blood. Before drinking it, I love to put my water in a glass bottle and charge it with inscriptions to make it as vibrant and supportive as possible. By doing this, I aim to change the vibration of all the water in my body, making it stronger and more intense. Do you find all this difficult to understand, Karoline?" Uncle Bernt asked. He realized he had totally gotten carried away. This was all so important to him, but Karoline was younger so she might not understand it all yet.

"Not to worry, Bernt," Grandma Gjertrud whispered softly, a loving look in her eyes. "Seems to me there is more than one Indigo in this house."

"I think a lot of what you said will have to go into my newly invented drawer for the time being," Karoline replied. "But I would really love to have a bottle like you just described. Adding to my body's vibrational powers by drinking vibrationally coded water sounds really cool."

"That is easily made," Uncle Bernt replied, happy that she seemed interested. "You just write a note and stick it on the bottle, or paint directly onto the bottle if you have some paint you can use."

"Oh, Uncle Bernt!" Karoline interrupted. "You must come to look at the paintings I made with Grandma Gjertrud yesterday!" The mention of paint had reminded her of yesterday's adventure and she was thrilled that Uncle Bernt would be the first to look at her creations.

"Will you show me?" Uncle Bernt asked, smiling. As he was about to walk out the door, he stopped and turned to Grandma Gjertrud. "Don't you have some painting to show me too, love?" he said, reaching for her hand. Grandma Gjertrud blushed, but immediately rose up and put her hand in Uncle Bernt's. All three of them went out to the lecture room.

"So when are you planning to start giving classes?" Uncle Bernt asked, after having thoroughly studied the paintings." You could easily fit at least five students in this room and they would be very fortunate to have you teaching them. This is really brilliant work!"

"I hadn't thought of that," said Grandma Gjertrud thoughtfully, and a smile started to spread over her face. "That would be wonderful!" Karoline said, looking eagerly at Grandma Gjertrud. "I could be your assistant and help you prepare the paper and painting plates!"

"Perfect timing, I guess!" Grandma Gjertrud grinned.

Bedtime Story Number Thirteen

"Can I make a comment about yesterday?" Karoline asked Grandma Gjertrud as they drove to Karoline's piano lesson the next afternoon. It was quite far away and they had both agreed it would be a perfect time for some secret talks.

"Of course, honey. You can always ask me whatever you want. Although I don't necessarily have time to answer right away, I will always get back to you as soon as I can. Never forget that. Now what did you want to talk about?"

"You know when we experimented throwing two stones in the water at one time, trying to see which stone would make waves strong enough to overpower the waves from the other stone?"

"Yes… "

"Well, twice in a row Samuel's stone made waves much stronger than mine. When I looked at the tiny waves being produced by my stone, I felt like those rings were *me*. I feel like this a lot when I'm with other people. It's like I forget what I want, or I don't want anything at all for myself. Being reminded that I was so weak even my little brother could easily conquer me made me really sad, but then Uncle Bernt told me what Samuel had already learned – that I could easily make my stone's waves stronger and more vibrant by putting more power into throwing it. When I did that, my stone's waves easily competed with Samuel's and it made me feel so great. Can I make my own inner vibrations or waves stronger, so that I don't feel so easily overwhelmed or influenced by others?"

"This is a very interesting topic, Karoline," Grandma Gjertrud said. "Let me start by commenting on the experiments that you did yesterday. When you stopped, you were still at a stage where you were looking to create waves that could conquer the other person's waves. Had you continued to experiment, you would have discovered that it is actually possible to create two more or less identical waves. As these two waves meet, they will not conquer each other. Instead they will merge as they meet, creating new kind of waves in the space between them. When we talk about people developing their inner vibrational potential, this is what we aim for; being able to create new and creatively inspiring vibrational fields between us as we deal with other people. This is how real peace is possible."

"Huh," Karoline said thoughtfully. She was almost moved to tears thinking how much she would love to have relationships like that with her friends. "But are you saying that for this to happen, we must all adjust our vibrational strength, making sure not to conquer someone else?"

"That is a really important question, Karoline," Grandma Gjertrud said. She was beginning to get really excited herself, as this was one of her absolute favorite topics. "Let's say my vibrational power is greater than yours – my waves are stronger. I could reduce my power to match yours making it possible for us to mingle in a nice way for you, but can you see any other solution?"

"You could always keep your vibration strong and offer me help to increase my own vibration. That would also be a way to make our vibrational strengths mingle in the end."

"That is right, honey," Grandma Gjertrud said. "Can you tell me which of these solutions you would prefer and why?"

"I don't know, Grandma Gjertrud! That is my problem. I told you that already!" Karoline said angrily. She was beginning to feel like a failure again.

"I am sorry, Karoline. It's my fault for not explaining this more clearly," Grandma Gjertrud replied hurriedly. "Let's leave this and come back to it later. Now I will try to answer your original question. You wanted to know if you could strengthen your inner vibration so you don't feel so easily overwhelmed by other people. I think you probably noticed the other day that even thinking about having a strong vibration made you feel strong and enthusiastic and happy inside. Am I right?"

"Yes," said Karoline uncertainly. "Go on." She felt a bit unsure if this was leading anywhere helpful, but still wanted to give it a chance.

"Let me start my answer with a question. If you think about what has happened this week, are there any situations where you have felt that your inner vibrations were strong enough to give you that same feeling?" Grandma Gjertrud asked. She could barely hide her excitement.

"Well, let me see…," Karoline started to think. "While I was doing that exercise, walking quickly with my back straight, I got a good and strong feeling inside."

"Good," said Grandma. "Any other situations?"

"When I ate my lunch after not eating all day at school, I also got a feeling of having more power, and when I managed to write my book review properly I felt like I ruled the whole world! Not to mention when I realized that painting was actually fun; that I could make things that expressed my own feelings like the waves and the tree. Somehow though, I still don't feel that I can hear my Inner Voice."

"This is great, Karoline!" Grandma Gjertrud exclaimed. "You have felt great several times in the last few days and feeling great always increases our vibration. You have noticed that eating when you had not eaten for a while made you feel great; that deliberately deciding how you want to move can change your mood for the better or the worse, depending on your posture; that learning how to master something new, like writing the book review, would make you feel great, but tell me, did you feel great when we started to talk about your book review, too?"

"No, I was rather angry at first when you started to talk about that." Karoline admitted.

"That was my impression, too," Grandma Gjertrud nodded. "You see, learning how to master new skills feels really good and increases your vibration, but to get there you might have to struggle a bit, feeling weak or uncomfortable along the way. What you need to understand is that if you only do the things that immediately make you feel great, thinking that this is the best ways to increase your vibration, you might miss the much more powerful and more satisfying feeling that comes from mastering something new. What was the last thing you said, though, honey?"

"I guess I complained that I still couldn't hear my Inner Voice." Karoline answered.

"How do you mean, exactly?"

"Well, the evening you taught me how to roll out my carpet and ask for help and guidance, I asked about what to say when I talked to Anne the next day, but I can't see that I've had any help on that at all, can you?"

"I see," said Grandma Gjertrud. She hesitated. "First I think we need to establish that your Inner Voice is not necessarily a voice that you can hear talking inside you, although some people do experience that. It has more to do with being in contact with yourself and feeling confident in being you. Now you think that because you still don't know what to say to Anne tomorrow, it means your request for help was not heard, but what *do* you know now Karoline, that you did not know last week?"

"I know a lot more about what I like," Karoline began. "And I know I need to strengthen myself and my inner vibrations to avoid feeling overwhelmed by others."

"Can you use this knowledge to help you find out what to say to Anne, do you think?"

"Probably," Karoline answered, "But I don't see how."

"Okay, let's try again. What does Anne want from you?" Grandma Gjertrud struggled to find the right way of explaining.

"She wants me to choose between her and my other friends," Karoline said.

"Okay, now we know what *she* wants, but what do *you* want, Karoline?" Grandma Gjertrud asked.

"I don't know, really," Karoline said. "I just don't want to have to choose."

"Great!" Grandma Gjertrud was thrilled. "You don't want to have to choose. Now you know that! So if you and Anne were throwing stones, her waves would say that you had to choose, and your waves would say that you didn't want to have to choose. What do you think would happen as the two waves meet?"

"I guess that would depend on how the two of us threw our stones," Karoline said. She liked the stone analogy. It made sense to her.

"That's right!" Grandma Gjertrud said. "So what would you have to do for your waves to meet in the middle?"

"I would have to throw my stone just as hard as Anne." Karoline sounded surprised as she heard the answer come out of her mouth. "Are you trying to make me understand, Grandma Gjertrud, that by increasing my inner strength, I will be perfectly capable of not only feeling what I want, but also knowing what to say to Anne tomorrow?"

"I am," Grandma Gjertrud replied. "And what have you been doing these past few days?"

"Working on my inner strength," Karoline replied.

"Do you think there is any chance that this might have to do with the fact that you asked for help, that you gave the Universe an invitation to assist you? What I want you to understand is that using the carpet exercise might help you in ways you don't expect, so if you ever use it again, be open to receiving help in any way that feels right to you. And here we are," Grandma Gjertrud said, parking the car. "Off you go to your piano lesson, Karoline. I will wait for you here. Enjoy yourself!"

"What did you mean when you said to Uncle Bernt yesterday that there was more than one Indigo in our house?" Karoline climbed into the car and fastened her seatbelt upon finishing her piano lessons. She had been meaning to ask this all day and couldn't wait any longer for the answer.

"Nothing passes you unnoticed, does it?" Grandma Gjertrud said. She gave Karoline a heartfelt smile and winked at her while starting the engine.

"The term 'Indigo Children' refers to certain children born in the second half of the twentieth century. Researchers started noticing that more and more children seemed to have unusually well-developed minds and spirits, and people who can see auras reported that the auras of these children were dominated by the color indigo. Indigo Children seem to have certain things in common. They tend to be empathetic, intuitive, highly intelligent and spiritually gifted, although not necessarily interested in spirituality. They can also be strong willed and often refuse to adapt to rigidity and authority. Most of all they often seem to be experienced and wise from a young age, something that might very well irritate their parents and teachers. If these children are not properly understood and treated respectfully by their parents or teachers, and especially if they are being lied to, they will often develop negative thoughts and feelings of hopelessness. Many suffer learning disabilities and lately many have been wrongly diagnosed with ADHD, ADD and autism."

"Do you think I am an Indigo Child?" Karoline stuttered. She felt a bit overwhelmed, but at the same time she felt like something was lighting up deep inside her. "I don't do well with authority, that's for sure," she said, giggling.

"And you are working your way through your feeling of hopelessness," Grandma Gjertrud added. "Yes, I certainly think that you are an Indigo Child, and I am excited to see how powerful your inner vibration will get now that you have decided to strengthen it."

"Are you also an Indigo person, Grandma Gjertrud?" Karoline said, although a bit scared this might be too personal a question.

"I believe I am," Grandma Gjertrud replied.

"Do I know anyone else who's an Indigo?"

"Are you thinking of someone in particular, Karoline?" Grandma Gjertrud asked. She was not going to give out this kind of information easily.

"Uncle Bernt?" Karoline suggested. She knew at once she was right, noticing the big smile on Grandma Gjertrud's lips.

When they arrived at home, Grandma Gjertrud reached into her bag and pulled out a pink, rose scented candle. She handed it to Karoline.

"I bought this for you, honey," she said. "I wanted you to know that I believe in your ability to find your own vibration and make your own decisions. Whenever you feel like it you can sit down to relax, light this candle, breathe deeply and look into the flame while you listen inwards and try to notice how you feel. Always remember, peace starts with you finding your inner space."

Karoline could feel tears forming behind her eyes. She was deeply moved by Grandma Gjertrud's words and gave her a big hug before leaving the car and heading for her room, holding her pink candle carefully in her hands.

Bedtime Story Number Fourteen

Karoline finished her tea and put the cup down on the breakfast table. "Can I invite some friends over for tacos tomorrow?" she asked. Hilde and Henrik glanced at each other in surprise. "Sure you can!" Hilde rallied. "What a great idea! I would love to meet your new friends. It might be a bit difficult with Olaf and Samuel around, though, and your room is a bit of a mess just now. Where could you eat, I wonder?"

"Well, I was planning on tidying my room this afternoon actually, so maybe we could eat in there after all," Karoline replied.

"If you want some help in the tidying business, I would be happy to help you," Grandma Gjertrud said.

"Oh, would you really, Grandma Gjertrud?" Karoline asked, delightedly. "I would love to have you help me. Thank you so much!"

"When do we start?" Grandma Gjertrud said.

"How about this afternoon, after school? I'll have a quick snack when I get in, just to make sure my energy lasts until dinner, then we can get started. With any luck we'll be done in time for Friday evening's taco and television night! Does that sound alright?"

"Sure does! I will be waiting for you this afternoon."

Grandma Gjertrud had some soup ready when Karoline came home from school. She had used homemade broth, hokkaido squash and nutmeg, mixing it thoroughly so it formed a smooth, orange-colored soup that she served with roasted pumpkin seeds.

"This tastes really good," Karoline said. She was grateful both for the soup and for the fact that Grandma Gjertrud had offered to help her tidy up her room.

"Grandma Gjertrud," Karoline said as she finished eating. "I want to make some changes in my room, but I am not sure how I would like it to be. Can you help me figure it out?"

"I would love to try, honey," Grandma Gjertrud replied. "Tell me about what you want in your life at the moment. The outer world can affect how we feel, so it's smart to plan your house or home in a way that will support the vibrational powers that you want to express. Did I manage to explain this so you can actually understand it?"

"What I hear is you saying that I need to align my room with my intentions for my own life. Is that what you meant?" Karoline asked.

"My meaning exactly," Grandma Gjertrud laughed. "You really understood me well, but you were much better than me in explaining it. Good job, honey!"

"So I'm back to having to describe what I want in my life," Karoline said thoughtfully. "What changes do I want?" She was more or less talking to herself. "I want to be more in charge of my life. I do not want to be overwhelmed by others as easily as I was before. I want to have more friends; friends that I can invite home to my room. I want my friends to feel comfortable when they visit me. I want people to see me as a cool, caring, self-confident teenager. I would also like to show people that I have my own personality, and that I am not like anybody else."

"I say that is quite an order for one day's work," Grandma Gjertrud commented. "Do you agree it would be smart to make an action plan on how to proceed with this operation?"

"Perfect suggestion," Karoline replied. "I will get a pen and paper."

Karoline could already feel joy building up inside just by talking about what she wanted for her life and for her room.

"This is *so* exciting, Grandma Gjertrud! Do you have any suggestions on how we should do this?"

"Yes, I do," Grandma Gjertrud said firmly. "I've reorganized quite a few rooms in my time and I've come up with a four-point plan. There are many more thorough ways of doing this, but I think this one will work well for now. The rest you can always learn later."

"Sounds great to me," said Karoline.

They sat at Karoline's desk and Grandma Gjertrud explained her four-point plan as Karoline made notes.

"Point Number One," she said. "Get rid of the clutter. Go through all your belongings and separate them into four groups: Use it, love it, give it away, and dump it. I like to use four, big cardboard boxes, one for each group. It makes this process easier and quicker."

"Point Number Two: Clean the room thoroughly with the vacuum cleaner, with soap and water, with your mind, and with incense or room spray."

"Point Number Three – Rearrange the things you have decided to keep."

"Point Number Four – Consider what new things to bring into the room and make a priority list."

"What do you think, Karoline? Any questions?"

"I love the fact there is such a list and I think these four steps sounds like a smart way to do the job," Karoline stated. "I do have some questions, though. In Point Number One, what do you mean by *clutter* and *love it*."

"Let me see." Grandma Gjertrud thought for a moment. "By 'clutter' I mean overcrowded, having too many things in one place, especially things that aren't used anymore. When things are not used their vibration gets slow and dull, and this tends to lower the vibration in the room. This means you have to work harder to keep your own inner vibration high while you're in such a room. Do you understand?"

"Sounds cool to me."

"By 'love it'," Grandma Gjertrud continued, "I mean that you might find things you don't use anymore, but which still mean a lot to you, and it would feel wrong to get rid of them. These kinds of things you can always put into a box and store in the attic. Some of the 'love it' things may even be so precious to you that you might want to put them somewhere in your room where you can enjoy looking at them every day."

"Okay, great," Karoline said. "Under Point Number Two, what do you mean by 'cleaning the room with my thoughts?' Isn't that pretty weird?"

"Yes, I see what you mean, but if you think about it, Uncle Bernt told you the other day that people could change the vibration in water by thinking about it, not even touching it. Being a human is a great responsibility. Even your thoughts may have an impact on a physical level. This means you will have to learn to master your thoughts, focusing on what you want to manifest and nothing else. There's no point in using lots of energy to clear out clutter and clean your room if the whole time you're feeling bitter, resentful, and discontented. Also, the more you work on increasing your vibration, the more damage your negative thoughts will be able to manifest."

"Good grief! That's a frightening thought. Right, so I need to fill my head with good thoughts while I'm cleaning my room. I need to think about how lovely it's going to look, and how much fun I'll have with my friends here once it's done. I think I'll listen to my favorite music while I work. That always cheers me up!"

"Good idea," Grandma Gjertrud said. "Any other questions?"

"Nope, I am ready to go," Karoline replied. "But do we have any suitable cardboard boxes?"

"There are some up in the attic. Will you fetch them, Karoline?"

"Already on my way!"

Karoline and Grandma Gjertrud started off clearing out the clutter with lots of energy. There were many things that had not been used for a while and Karoline had to work hard on deciding which things to keep, which things to give away, and which things to throw away. A lot of her clothes and toys were no longer useful, but they still had some emotional effect on her. In spite of this attachment, she managed to fill a couple of garbage bags with things she was happy to get rid of.

When they were finally finished with Points Number One and Two, they took a little break to sit down. That's when Karoline suddenly said, "I told Anne about your painting class today and she said she would love to come. When are we going to start?"

Grandma Gjertrud was taken totally by surprise at this. "That sounds great," she finally managed to say. "We already have our first customer. I guess we will have to make an information sheet and put it up at the store, don't you think?"

"I think we should paint the background of the paper before we write on it. That will make a great impression and show everyone what this is all about," Karoline answered.

Grandma Gjertrud suddenly started laughing. Karoline smiled, but looked a bit puzzled. After a minute she said, "Grandma Gjertrud, what are you laughing at?"

"I'm laughing at your old grandmother," Grandma Gjertrud said.

"What have you done that is so funny?"

"I have just realized what a great girl you are, and what a clumsy grandmother I am."

"Okay, now I'm confused. What on earth do you mean?" asked Karoline.

"Well, last week you told me how Anne had demanded you choose between her and your other friends by today. I've spent the whole week wondering how best to support you in finding your own way solution, and today was the day you would give her your conclusion. This morning you asked for permission to invite some friends over tomorrow, meaning you must have decided to continue seeing them, meaning you might be hurting Anne's feelings by saying no to her. Then you tell me she is happy to come join our painting class. So now everybody seems to be happy but me, who cannot yet figure out what has happened. Can you see why I feel like an old, slow-moving turtle?"

Karoline could not help but burst out laughing and Grandma Gjertrud soon joined her.

"I'm sorry I didn't think to tell you, Grandma Gjertrud," Karoline said when she stopped laughing.

"You must think I don't realize how much you've been helping me this week. I do, and I appreciate it very much. I was so glad to wake up this morning knowing exactly what I wanted to do. I wanted to be together with my new friends, feeling just as good as I did in the beginning, but I also wanted to spend some time with Anne, now and then, as we have known each other for so long. So I told her that and then I mentioned the painting class you had given me and how we were going to arrange painting classes for others soon. That's when she said she had always wanted to learn how to paint and could she please join our class!"

"I'm truly amazed Karoline," Grandma Gjertrud stuttered. "What a great decision! You must feel so proud having produced this great outcome."

"No. The decision itself came to me in my dreams, so that was the easiest part. Working on increasing my vibration has been quite an experience, though. Thank you so much for helping me with this, Grandma Gjertrud! I am so happy inside. I feel like I could go on and clean the entire house!"

After putting Karoline's remaining things back in order, they sat down again and made notes on what kinds of items Karoline would like to bring into her room now that it was clean and tidy.

"I love these little ornaments and things and would like to keep them in my room," Karoline said, "But I don't want to have to move each of them every time I clean."

"I suggest you find a nice plate or a tray where you can arrange them all in, and then instead of moving each object, you only have to move the tray. If you have many such objects you can even consider circulating them between the tray and a box that you keep in your desk. What kind of tray or plate would you like? Maybe we can find something elsewhere in the house," Grandma Gjertrud suggested.

They found an old silver-colored circular tray that Karoline adored and soon all her small objects - an angel, dolphin, dragon, a beautiful gemstone, and the little pink candle, all fit perfectly on the tray.

When the room was finished, Grandma Gjertrud went to take a shower and Karoline sat down to enjoy her vibrant new room before joining the rest of her family, and waiting for her friends who were coming over for tacos.

Later that evening she thought *"This has been the best week of my life,"* as she lit her little, pink candle to reflect about all she had learned.

Grandma Gjertrud's Third Visit

Karoline's Life at Thirty-Six

Karoline shut the front door behind her, put down her bags and sighed. Another long day at work. She pulled a small parcel out of her handbag and quickly opened it, revealing a pink candle. It smelled of roses. Holding it to her nose and smiling she went up to her bedroom. She'd decided that she needed help with the problems she'd been having with her new boss, and now she knew how to ask for that help. Lighting the candle, she breathed deeply and rolled out a carpet in her mind representing her problems. Within a short time she found herself imagining sparkles of colored energy raining down on it.

It had already been a week since Grandma Gjertrud's last visit, and Karoline felt both excited and a little nervous as bedtime approached. As she sat in bed waiting, the little church bell on her bedside table jingled slightly, and there was Grandma Gjertrud again, standing by the door.

"Oh, Grandma Gjertrud I really love these stories," Karoline sighed happily. "It's frightening the way small things can have such a big impact on our lives, isn't it? If I hadn't locked my bedroom door that evening, or if you had insisted on coming in rather than hesitating, my life might have been quite different. How you deal with things and solve everyday problems is so important, especially when you work with other people. As a teacher, the things I do and say can really affect people's lives and I need to take that responsibility seriously."

"I totally agree," Grandma Gjertrud said. "I'm so sorry I didn't wait just a little longer and listen to my intuition before I left your door that night, Karoline."

"But that's part of life too, isn't it?" Karoline said thoughtfully. "There are so many hundreds of small decisions to make every day. All you can do is what seems like the best thing at the time and trust that things will work out as they're meant to be. If you tried to predict the outcome of every little decision you'd go mad!"

Grandma Gjertrud chuckled. "I suppose you're right," she said. "My wise granddaughter can still teach me a thing or two!"

"It's a shame my real life didn't go the same way as the bedtime story Karoline's," Karoline said sadly. "But I'm so grateful to be learning all this stuff now. It feels good to be in control of my emotions and to feel my vibration getting stronger and stronger. I feel like I'm learning and growing along with bedtime story Karoline, and for the first time in years I'm really starting to feel like things might work out for me."

"Oh Karoline," Grandma Gjertrud replied. "I'm so glad to hear that, and it warms my heart to see you smile again, even if only for short moments at this stage."

"You will help me with the rest of my problems as well, won't you Grandma Gjertrud?"

Karoline suddenly felt mild panic rise in her. Yes, she was doing better, but she wasn't ready to do without Grandma Gjertrud help just yet.

"Of course I will, honey," Grandma Gjertrud assured her. "I can promise you one last round of seven bedtime stories and a final session together after that. What do you want me to look at this time?"

"There are two main things really," said Karoline. "One is my boyfriend and the other is my health."

"Can you tell me more about them?" Grandma Gjertrud asked. "How are these areas troubling you?"

"How are they *not* troubling me?" Karoline muttered. "Right. First let's talk about my boyfriend, Hans. We met four years ago. I was still a bit wary of men as my previous boyfriend was a real jerk… " Karoline looked out the window for a moment, thinking. "I was cautious of getting involved, but Hans managed to charm his way into my heart. He moved in with me after a year and we have lived together since. I had just started referring to him as my "husband" when he told me two weeks ago that he didn't like how our relationship had developed. He claimed I was holding back, but I always felt like *he* was the one holding back: working all the time, giving speaking lectures, and travelling abroad a lot. I really love him, but I don't know if I can trust him. As soon as I start relaxing, letting down my guard and thinking this is really going to work, off he goes and I don't see him for weeks. And now he has threatened to leave me. I don't know what to do. I'm so scared. I don't think I could survive another breakup."

"Okay," said Grandma Gjertrud. "Tell me a bit more about your previous boyfriend. It seems to me that if we understand what happened then, it might help us understand the problems you're having with Hans now."

Karoline took a deep breath. "Peter was my first big love," she started slowly. "I gave him everything – heart, soul and body – and we were so happy together. We were with each other night and day and it was wonderful. We both studied to become teachers and lived in a small flat together with another couple. The four of us would often go on holidays and weekends away together, and we ate dinner together every night of the week. After a year or two we both had good jobs and we moved into a flat on our own. Everything was fine until I started to talk about us having a baby. I thought having a child would be the normal next step to take, but he didn't seem to agree. Suddenly he started to go out more, worked longer hours, and refused to talk to me when I tried to find out what was happening. Then one day he told me he was moving out. He'd been having an affair with the girl we used to share a flat with and she was pregnant. He'd decided to make his life with her and the baby. I was totally shocked. I felt so rejected and hurt. I didn't see how I could ever recover."

"Is that what had happened when you came to see me that summer?" Grandma Gjertrud asked.

"Yes," Karoline admitted. "I know I told you a totally different version. I gave you the impression I was the one who walked out on him. I just couldn't admit to anyone that he'd given my best friend the baby he knew I wanted so dearly. I am sorry I misled you, Grandma Gjertrud."

"Oh honey," Grandma Gjertrud replied. "I must have been such an idiot not to see that there was more to it than you told me. We sure need to look deeper into this one. But you were worried about your health as well. What is that all about?"

"I don't know what's the matter with me. I went to the doctor for my regular check-up and then a week or so ago I got this strange letter saying there was something abnormal in my blood work and asking me to come back next week. I'm so scared, Grandma Gjertrud. I'm sure I've got some awful cancer or something, but what scares me most is that I don't seem to care. It's like I welcome the disease and almost look forward to dying. Admittedly I've been feeling a bit better about that since you've been here, but still... I don't know what to think."

"Okay honey, we'll work on that too," Grandma Gjertrud said gently. "In my stories this week I'll focus on when you came to see me that summer, after you broke up with your first boyfriend. Does that sound good to you, Karoline?"

"It does," Karoline whispered. "But will you promise to stay until I fall asleep?"

"I promise," said Grandma Gjertrud. "You snuggle down and get comfortable."

Grandma Gjertrud started humming as she tucked the bedcovers safely around her girl.

PART THREE

Karoline's Life at Twenty-six

Bedtime Story Number Fifteen

K aroline's voice sounded flat and emotionless when Grandma Gjertrud answered the phone. "Can I come to visit you for a few days?" she asked.

She had hardly slept last night, crying and shouting out into the darkness of her bedroom, "How could he do this to me! That bastard! Cheating on me with my best friend! Making her pregnant, even! Giving her the child he was never willing to give to me!" She had turned the matter over and over in her head, but always ending up blaming herself for not having seen this coming. "I gave him everything!" she cried.

"Being with him was all I wanted and look where that got me!" In the early hours of the morning a new thought had joined the others: "People are going to hear about this. They're going to know! Oh no, not that! I can't stand people pitying me, feeling sorry for me plus all their curious questions!" Then she had an idea. She used to have good conversations with God when she was a little girl. There hadn't been much need for those kinds of talks lately, not since that wonderful boy had walked into her life when she was sixteen. Maybe it was time to open up the lines of communication again. *Oh God,* she thought ardently. *I just can't face everyone after what's happened. Please get me out of here.* But much to her surprise, God gave her no sign that He was listening.

For the past ten years her whole life had been full of Peter. It had been obvious to her from the beginning that this was the man she was going to spend her whole life with. They went to University together, lived together, shared whatever friends, money, and possessions they had as well. They both found jobs at the same school (although their departments and specializations were different), and eventually they bought a house. And then she had suggested they should have a baby. "What was so wrong with that?" she kept asking herself as the early summer dawn started to creep across the hills she could see in the distance from her bedroom window. "I need to get away for a few days, to think, but where can I go? I hardly have any money. Oh my God, the house! He kicked me out of our house! I don't even have a home! I have to be out by the end of next week because *he* needs the house more than I do since he has a family to support." This thought made her feel sick to her stomach. She lay tormenting herself until the sun had risen mid-way in the summer sky and then she suddenly remembered. *Grandma Gjertrud!* She could go see Grandma Gjertrud! That's when she made the call.

"Oh, Karoline, I would love to have you come visit us!" Grandma Gjertrud sounded thrilled. "When are you coming, honey?"

"Can I come this afternoon?"

"Sure you can come this afternoon." Grandma Gjertrud hesitated a moment, then said, "Honey, is there something wrong?"

Karoline's voice sounded strained as she tried not to cry, but she managed to say, "No. It's just that I decided to break up with Peter and I have to be out the house by next week. I thought it would be nice to spend a few days with you before I think about finding somewhere new to live."

"Well, it'll be lovely to see you," Grandma Gjertrud said warmly. "We'll have plenty of time to chat over herbal tea and cookies, and go for walks, just like the old days. You just come and relax for a while. Call when you know which train you will be on and we will be there at the station waiting for you."

As she put down the phone, Karoline realized the new truth that had now been established. *She* was leaving *him*, not the other way around. "When in Rome, do as the Romans do…" she told herself. Everyone else seemed to cheat. Why shouldn't she?

"Over here, Karoline!" Grandma Gjertrud shouted from the platform at the train station the next day. She had immediately spotted Karoline as she'd stepped out of the train and now she waved from outside the car to attract her attention.

She looks so sad and vulnerable, this honey of mine, Grandma Gjertrud thought to herself, *and so much older than her twenty-six years. I can see from all the way over here that she's not happy. Her hair is dull, her skin looks grey, her clothes are badly fitted, and her shoes are boring. She looks miserable, but why is she miserable if she is the one who's decided to leave her boyfriend? Why isn't she relieved and happy?*

"Grandma Gjertrud, how great to see you," Karoline said, as she was immediately pulled into a warm hug. Then she noticed Uncle Bernt, leaning against the car.

"Uncle Bernt!" she exclaimed, and ran over to greet him too. "What a pleasant surprise to find you're paying Grandma Gjertrud a visit too!"

"Got to look after my darling, you know," Uncle Bernt said. "Only this time I have come to stay."

Karoline didn't notice Uncle Bernt's remark at first. She was too preoccupied preparing her story, making sure that even Grandma Gjertrud wouldn't be able to tell that it was a pack of lies.

The car finally stopped outside the farmhouse and Karoline climbed out and stretched. It was a lovely summer afternoon, and she soon took off her jacket and was surprised to feel the sun warming her skin. Two big geese strutted by, followed by their goslings.

"How cute they are!" Karoline said. "We never had geese when I lived here, did we?"

"No," Grandma Gjertrud answered, "But I have always wanted some so last year I decided to treat myself to a couple. They are such friendly creatures, this particular kind of geese."

"And beautiful too," Karoline added.

"But I must admit they honk a lot. Whenever people arrive here, the geese make sure to tell me about it."

Later that evening, the three of them sat together on the terrace having dinner.

"What did you mean about coming here to stay, Uncle Bernt?" Karoline suddenly asked.

"So you *did* actually hear what I said!" Uncle Bernt smiled. "I thought you weren't listening."

"Isn't it wonderful?" Grandma Gjertrud said happily. "Now that even Samuel has moved out and your parents have gone off to spend the whole summer sailing in the Mediterranean, I started to feel lonely living on the farm all by myself."

"So I offered to come here as her gardener," Uncle Bernt filled in. "But you can't really trust gardeners these days, can you?" He smiled. "Finally, she gave in and agreed to be my girlfriend."

"I was taken by surprise," Grandma Gjertrud commented.

"That's when I proposed," Uncle Bernt said. "And do you know what she answered?"

"Yes, I hope!" Karoline laughed. When nobody replied she continued. "You did say yes, Grandma Gjertrud, didn't you? Tell me you did!"

"I said he would have to give me a week to consider it," Grandma Gjertrud said finally.

"Can you imagine? There he is, my prince, chevalier, rescuer, and soulmate, and when he offers to marry me, something I have been dreaming of all these years, I need a whole week to make up my mind!" Grandma Gjertrud couldn't hold back her laughter anymore.

"You're kidding me, right?" Karoline asked. "You didn't do that, Grandma Gjertrud. You didn't hurt his feelings like that, did you?"

"I'm afraid I did."

"But what if he had chosen to walk out on you when you treated him like that?"

"Guess that would have shown me he wasn't my type after all," Grandma Gjertrud laughed.

"No, to be honest, I asked for a week to think over his proposal, but after a couple of hours of listening inwards, increasing my vibrations, and then a nice, long bath with salt and scented oils and some great wine, I *knew* I had made up my mind."

"Can you imagine my feelings as she called me that evening to say '*I will*?'" Uncle Bernt grinned. "I must be the luckiest guy in the world!"

"When did all this happen?" Karoline asked. She was surprised they had not told her earlier.

"Yesterday!" Grandma Gjertrud replied.

Karoline was so surprised to see the two of them holding each other's hands while talking, teasing each other when telling their story and smiling a lot. Most of all she was amazed by the whole atmosphere, not only there on the terrace, but all over the farm. It was as if the whole place was welcoming her. She could feel her frozen heart starting to melt, when The Thought struck her again. "He cheated on me, that bastard!"

It was getting late. The last of the wine had been drunk and it was starting to get chilly. "I made up a bed for you in your old bedroom, Karoline," Grandma Gjertrud said. "I hope you don't mind sharing the room with my sewing machines and piles of fabric. Last Christmas I got so fed up with never getting sparkling clothes in my size I decided to start making my own. It's fascinating how some seemingly plain fabric can turn into a great creation. It's simply magical – and I love it!"

"Oh good. I was hoping you would give me my old room," Karoline replied. "And sewing machines and fabric are fine. I'm just so happy to be here."

As they made their way up the stairs, Grandma Gjertrud suddenly turned to Karoline and said "I can tell you're lying, Karoline. I am okay with you not wanting to tell me things, but I do *not* allow lies in my house. You have no idea how crippling lies can be." She looked deep into Karoline's eyes, but much to Karoline's surprise Grandma Gjertrud's eyes did not transmit anger in any way. They were filled with love and acceptance.

"I'm sorry, Grandma Gjertrud," Karoline said sheepishly. "I should have known you wouldn't just take my word for it. You always listen inwards before accepting things."

"Yes, I do, and I think it might be time for you to start doing that too, Karoline." Again Karoline was surprised that the firmness in Grandma Gjertrud's voice was not accompanied by any feeling of anger, just love. "I ask you, seriously, to wipe that cover story of yours out of your mind immediately, together with the thought that you needed one in the first place. You are welcome to take your time in accepting the real story, but no more lies. Am I making myself clear, Karoline? "

"Oh yes, you certainly are," Karoline answered.

"Good! While you make yourself comfortable in your room, let me get you some nice herbal tea to help you sleep," Grandma Gjertrud said. "I'll be back soon."

Karoline unpacked quickly, took a shower, and climbed into bed. She hoped she could have a chat with Grandma Gjertrud like they used to in the old days, and that Grandma would offer to tuck her in. That had always made her feel so safe and so loved.

Grandma Gjertrud came in with two mugs of tea and put them down on the bedside table.

"I am so glad to have you here, Karoline," she said, "Especially now that I have just said yes to marrying Uncle Bernt. It'll be so much more fun planning the wedding together with someone else. Would you mind helping me with that, honey?"

"I'd be delighted to Grandma Gjertrud," Karoline assured her. "It would be a honor." She could feel a lovely warm glow starting to spread inside her with all this talk of marriage. Even though The Thought threatened to start talking inside her head, she did not listen to it. In that instant she knew that she was lying in the right bed, in the right house, on the right day, and that made her feel very good indeed. "Perfect timing, Grandma Gjertrud!" she heard herself say as she smiled.

"Can you teach me how to listen inward, Grandma Gjertrud?" Karoline asked.

"I would be happy to, honey! But tonight I think you are too tired to do much work. Let me just show you a little peace exercise to increase your vibrations further by connecting to external sources of unlimited energy."

"Do you really think I can do that?" Karoline asked.

"Certainly, honey, otherwise I wouldn't have suggested it. If you sit up in your bed and make yourself comfortable, I will guide you through the exercise. Ready?"

"I am!"

"Close your eyes and start to breathe deeply. Think about something you love and really concentrate on how that feels in your body. Let that feeling grow."

"This is like the exercise you taught me when I was a little girl, isn't it?"

"It's almost the same. Now hush... Let the feeling grow bigger and bigger until it forms a bubble all around you. Now in your mind, reach up above your head and imagine stretching right up into the spaces where stars and galaxies are being formed. Grasp onto some of those magical vibrations and pull them down into your bubble."

Karoline pictured herself reaching out her hand, a look of concentration on her face.

"Now imagine pushing your toes so far into the earth that they splash into a lake of intense white light, sparkling brightly. Can you feel that white light coming up through your feet, your legs, and filling the bubble? Can you feel how all these vibrations mix so the inside of your bubble is now vibrating really intensely?"

"Yes!" Karoline giggled

"Great! Now let your bubble expand, filling the whole room, then filling the whole house, the farm, all of our community, our country, and at last, the whole planet, until you can picture yourself holding the whole planet in your arms. Are you okay with this so far?"

"I am."

"Now, start giving these vibrations as a gift to all the waters on the planet, to all the animals in the waters, to the skies and all the birds and insects, to all the animals on the planet, to all the trees and plants, and finally, to all the people living on the planet. As you feel you have connected to them all, send them an extra whoosh of vibrational energy before you come back to your body and then back to me in this room."

"Oh, that was awesome, Grandma Gjertrud. I was actually holding the whole planet in my arms! It felt so right. How can that be?" Karoline wondered.

"I'm not sure everything can be explained, Karoline, but I'm glad that you liked the exercise. Now I think you should lie down to sleep. I'm pretty sure you didn't sleep much last night."

Karoline blushed and snuggled down. As Grandma Gjertrud tucked her in she noticed that some color was beginning to come into Karoline's cheeks. "My darling, little apple fairy." she said. "Sweet dreams!" Then she started to hum an old lullaby and Karoline was soon fast asleep.

Bedtime Story Number Sixteen

"Last night you asked me to teach you how to listen inwards," Grandma Gjertrud said to Karoline at breakfast the next morning, "But to be honest, I am not sure there is much of interest to listen to inside your body for the time being. My impression is that your body is barely vibrating at the moment."

Karoline immediately started crying.

"Oh, I'm sorry, honey," Grandma Gjertrud said hurriedly. "I didn't mean to hurt your feelings. I was going to suggest that you and I could sit down with a pot of tea and some cookies and have a nice chat, as soon as I tidy up the kitchen a little. Uncle Bernt told me he is going to work out in the fields this morning so we'll have the place to ourselves. How about you make some nice tea and set the table outside? The weather is so nice and we can sit in front of the house and get rosy cheeks and some extra freckles," she said smiling all the while.

"That would be lovely!" Karoline replied. "Any special tea you would like?" But Grandma Gjertrud didn't seem to hear her, so she looked into the herb cupboard herself, smelling her way to a perfect mixture.

"I should try to explain my remark at the breakfast table, Karoline," Grandma Gjertrud said, pouring the tea.

"When people experience grief, they can react in many ways. Some people react spontaneously: they cry loudly and get a lot of feelings out straight away. Others hardly shed any tears at all and only want to show signs of grieving in private. Still others get angry, yelling, and feeling like they need to damage something. And then, of course, there are all the other ways of reacting. My point is it seems to me you are trying not to show your reactions. You have split up with Peter for some reason and here you are, not even wanting to talk about it."

"When people grieve, but don't allow themselves to react to that grief, they often end up closing off their hearts totally. Their vibrations get weaker and weaker until they're barely vibrating at all, and they find that they have no inner voice. In order for someone to be able to listen inwards, their heart must be open. The fact that you felt you needed a cover story makes me realize you also feel ashamed of something. But feelings like grief, shame, powerlessness, and guilt lower your vibration enormously, honey. It makes it much harder to take care of yourself, never mind learn how to hear your inner voice and learn to work with it."

"But what am I to do then, Grandma Gjertrud?" Karoline cried. "I need to get myself moving and find a way to solve this. I thought that by learning to listen inwards I would get some guidance about what I should do and stop everything from getting totally out of hand. Is that so bad?"

"But honey, I think things already are out of hand. Maybe you should try to face that? Or is that what this is all about?" Grandma Gjertrud stopped talking and waited for Karoline's reply.

"About me not wanting to face this, you mean?" Karoline said.

"Something like that."

"He gave my baby… to someone else!" Karoline blurted out, starting to cry. "To my best friend, even! Why? I gave him everything I had in me, for ten whole years. What did I do to deserve this?"

Grandma Gjertrud stretched out her hand and ran it through Karoline's hair, putting some of it behind

Karoline's ear and then caressing her cheek. "My darling Karoline," she said. "That must have been dreadful for you. What happened exactly?"

Karoline reached out and squeezed Grandma Gjertrud's hand tightly, sobbing and sobbing as she started to tell the whole story. The more she talked, the better she started to feel and gradually she stopped crying. They talked for hours with Grandma asking questions from time to time, helping Karoline to remember details she'd chosen to forget. The tea, untouched, went cold, but the morning sun got warmer and started to remove the grey shadows from Karoline's complexion. Grandma Gjertrud noticed that Karoline started to relax now that her story was out in the open, but she kept looking for signs that there might still be more that she needed to express. She also listened inwards for guidance on how to best proceed.

"If it is true that our body is the vessel of our Soul," Grandma Gjertrud said suddenly, "What kind of Soul is your body capable of carrying at the moment, Karoline?"

"I'm not sure that anyone would fancy living in my body at the moment," Karoline replied.

Grandma Gjertrud spotted the smile that was playing around Karoline's lips and felt assured that this would lead somewhere.

"Remember what I was saying earlier, about it being a problem to listen inwards if your heart is closed?" she said. "Before you can listen inwards, you must make sure there is something vibrating inside you so there will be something to listen to. You need to prepare your body for hosting higher vibrations, which in turn will make it safe for you to open yourself to love, to receiving God."

"But how can I do that?" Karoline asked.

"There are a lot of techniques and I believe you know some of them already, don't you?"

"Oh dear, now you're making me feel stupid," Karoline replied. "I don't seem to remember anything at all at the moment. Do you think it's me starting to get old, Grandma Gjertrud?"

"Definitely!" Grandma watched as Karoline started to laugh, carefully at first, but then with more confidence. Grandma laughed too.

"I believe Uncle Bernt once told you about vibrations in water and how that can affect your internal water. Do you remember that lesson?"

"Oh that's true. I do remember that." Karoline replied. "Are you saying I should drink some special water?"

"Yes, I think that would be a good idea. We have bottles inside and I'll show you later, but there are also other things that you can easily do to prepare your body for higher vibrations."

"Such as?" Karoline was beginning to get impatient. There were still some feelings inside of her that she wanted to get rid of.

"Well, changing your diet can help a lot, leaving out the foods that tend to cause problems such as wheat, milk products, and sugar, and adding some of the ones that come with the best vibrations, such as wild and raw foods, which, by the way, will be no problem while you are here as we eat that kind of diet. Exercise is another thing that can help, keeping your body moving and stretching, making your blood flow more freely. Meditation in any form, or just being by yourself for a while, lighting a candle, using some of the visualization techniques you already know, is highly beneficial too. And then you have cleansing yourself with salt to repair holes or leakages in your aura, making it easier to keep up your vibration without losing it to the surroundings. Plus there is also clearing out clutter and cleaning your room with thoughts, water, and incense. Hmm... did I forget anything?"

"But Grandma Gjertrud, these are all the tools that you taught me when I was a little girl! I forgot all about them! I haven't used them in years!" Karoline said, sounding surprised. "Are you telling me that my relationship would have been different if I'd applied these tools from the start?"

"No, no," Grandma Gjertrud said, waving her finger at Karoline. "Don't go there! Do not start to put yourself down again. We are working, here and now, making your future better than the past. There's no point in beating yourself up for nothing. That will just make you feel worse."

"Nothing!" Karoline shouted. "Are you calling ten years nothing? I stayed with Peter for ten years and during those years I totally forgot to use all these tools that you had given me as a child. I could have had a much better life if I'd remembered, but I didn't, so now I don't even have a boyfriend anymore,"

Karoline said angrily. "And you're telling me not to bother about that?"

"No," replied Grandma Gjertrud calmly. "I'm just telling you that beating yourself up is not going to help you to increase your vibrancy, and you wanted me to help you increase it so you could learn how to listen inwards, am I right?"

"Yes… but…" Karoline had to admit that Grandma was right, but she was still upset.

"Anger is great, Karoline. It gives you a lot of energy, but don't turn that anger against yourself. That is not going help you at all. If you feel like expressing anger, go chop some wood, or let it out by beating a pillow or something. Just promise me you will not beat on yourself. Now we need some food," Grandma Gjertrud said. "I can remember a girl coming home from school totally exhausted, having forgotten to eat her packed lunch. Was that you by any chance?" she said looking Karoline straight in the eye.

"Yes, that would have been me," she answered, smiling a little at the memory.

"Eating is essential for getting you back into shape," Grandma Gjertrud said. "Why don't you walk over to the field and ask Uncle Bernt to help you find some vegetables for lunch?"

"Yes, there must be plenty of good stuff growing in the garden by now," Karoline commented as she rose from her chair. She stretched a bit and then set off for the field, feeling like a young girl again.

After lunch, Karoline offered to help Grandma Gjertrud weed the flowerbeds around the house. It was fun revealing all the perennials, giving them more space to grow. Grandma Gjertrud also asked her to help put compost on the rose bushes, readying for a long and rich flowering season.

"I think you should start dating your Soul, Karoline," Grandma Gjertrud said.

"You think *what?*" Karoline said in surprise.

"It seems to me you and your Soul have not been talking much lately, and it might just be that your Soul has lost confidence in you in some way. That means you will have to earn that trust again."

"And how exactly would I do that?" Karoline asked.

"By showing some heartfelt interest, listening with great concern, and by being reliable, I guess," Grandma Gjertrud replied. "Imagine going on a date with a wonderful man, someone you think might become really special to you. Think of how you would behave to catch his interest and treat your Soul the same way."

"But how do I know if my Soul is responding?" Karoline asked.

"It could respond in many ways," Grandma Gjertrud answered. "Try to listen for any help, like something making you remember to make a phone call you almost forgot, to lock the door, or to turn off the oven, to suddenly remembering where to find something that you had been looking for. All these small voices that help you through the day and that you never thought of thanking. Start doing that now. Start believing in your Soul and the help it gives, and your Soul will start believing in you again, too."

Dear Soul, Karoline said to herself. *I'm sorry I haven't been listening much to you lately. Shall we go for a walk in the woods? Maybe we'll find some wild herbs to use in a smoothie.*

Karoline went off on her own and Grandma Gjertrud watched as her posture straightened and her movements quickened. She was already starting to vibrate again.

That evening Grandma Gjertrud helped Karoline put together a rich smoothie using the ingredients she'd picked in the woods and around the farm. "These lovely things will do you a world of good," she said, "And they'll also help you sleep soundly all night."

"That's exactly what I need," Karoline said, yawning. "I'm taking a bath with some salt before bed. It will be a perfect place to enjoy my smoothie."

When Grandma Gjertrud came to tuck Karoline in, she seemed to suddenly remember something. A smile started to spread across her face.

"You know, I've got a lot of old, chipped china sitting in the attic. I think what we both need is a fresh start. You with your new life without Peter and me marrying Uncle Bernt. Plus smashing that china might be a great way to get rid of all the old, stuck vibrations! I should really have a *polterabend,* or hen night, before I get married, so why don't we combine the two?"

"I'd love to!" Karoline replied. "I have always wanted to do something really naughty and this sounds like a great opportunity to get it all out!"

Bedtime Story Number Seventeen

"You keep talking about perfect timing, but what could possibly be the perfect timing in Peter leaving me?" Karoline asked Grandma Gjertrud in a rather irritated way the next morning.

"Yes, that's what I keep asking myself, too," Grandma Gjertrud replied. "Can you see anything beneficial about it?"

"He left me, that bastard, making me feel really worthless. How can that be beneficial to me at all? He gets to keep the house and I don't even know where I'm going to live."

"Are you asking for my opinion on this, or are you just telling me to feel sorry for you?" Grandma Gjertrud sounded like she was about to lose her patience, which was exactly what Karoline wanted her to do. Karoline was looking for someone to quarrel with, someone to criticize in order to make herself feel better.

"I'm not having this, Karoline," Grandma Gjertrud said firmly. "I am happy to help you when you are ready to look at your situation from a new perspective, but until then I have more important things to attend to." With that remark she rose from the breakfast table and left the room, leaving Karoline to tidy up.

She was almost finished when Uncle Bernt came in for his morning coffee.

"How are you today, sweetie?" he asked, pleased to have the company. "Did you have a good night's sleep?"

"Yes, I love sleeping in my old bed," Karoline answered. "I find that with all the beautiful fabric lying around in there, I keep dreaming of having new dresses in bright colors." As she mentioned it she could immediately feel her mood rising, making her smile inside.

"That's what your grandmother keeps telling me, too, and I must admit she looks great in bright colors. Nothing beats a lady wearing red, though," he said, smiling to himself.

"What made you decide to come and live with Grandma Gjertrud?" Karoline asked him.

"What makes you think it was my decision?" Uncle Bernt answered, winking at Karoline.

"Are you telling me *she* asked *you*?" Karoline said sounding shocked. Although Grandma Gjertrud had told her this, she hadn't altogether believed it. She thought that kind of decision was for the man to make.

"She sure did," Uncle Bernt replied. "If it wasn't for her I wouldn't have been living here now."

Karoline could not stop her jaw from dropping.

"I'm a shy man, you see, Karoline," he continued, "And I have never lived together with a woman before, much less asked a woman to marry me!" Thinking about the big changes he had just made in his life made Uncle Bernt smile.

"A woman can have such a great impact on a man, you see," he said. "There is hardly anything a man wouldn't do to make his woman smile. A true lady can make a man want to do his utmost every day, and here I am with two beautiful women in the house! Can you blame me for feeling extremely lucky and grateful? Nothing less than perfect timing is happening right now. I might just send a nice bunch of flowers to your parents, too, to thank them for going travelling this summer. If they hadn't done that, I'm not sure your

Grandma would have acted on her feelings and I wouldn't be sitting here now."

Karoline laughed. "Life is so full of surprises," she said. "Thank you for reminding me about that!"

Karoline decided that a walk was just the thing to clear her head so off she went into the field, picking flowers on this warm summer's day. She thought about her conversation with Uncle Bernt. What was it that he had said? *If it wasn't for her I wouldn't have been living here now.* He was saying it was the woman who decided how to proceed with their relationship. And what was the other thing he'd said? *A true lady can make a man want to do his utmost every day.* Karoline had never heard such thoughts being expressed before by a man. Realizing how important a woman's actions could be to a relationship puzzled her. Soon she had to ask herself the next logical question. *What was my role in my relationship? What decisions did I make, and when did I inspire Peter to "do his utmost?"* Quickly realizing that the answer to that last question was "never," she quickly turned around and started to walk back home with quick steps. She was ready to face Grandma Gjertrud again.

"I'd like to try looking at my relationship from a new angle. Will you help me?" she said to Grandma Gjertrud who was in the kitchen preparing lunch.

"Of course I will, honey!" Grandma Gjertrud answered. "But first, please forgive me for being so harsh with you this morning. It wasn't nice of me."

"Oh, that's alright. I should really thank you. It helped me see things differently, and I've been thinking about things. Can you help me figure out what my role was in my relationship with Peter and why our breakup happened?"

"I can see that you have been working hard already on finding the answers," Grandma Gjertrud said smiling. She sounded impressed and that made Karoline feel proud.

"Tell me something about your relationship, Karoline," Grandma Gjertrud began. "Tell me about your dreams and intentions and what it was that made you think Peter was the right man for you."

Karoline became overwhelmed with emotion. She ran her hands through her hair trying to figure out how to answer that question. "I'm not sure I had any dreams or intentions, to be honest. Does that sound weird?"

"Not at all, Karoline. I hear that often. People end up in relationships they just fell into; no dreams, no intentions, no big expectations. And then when the relationship breaks, they suddenly feel they have lost something and start fighting to get it back. But they never think to ask themselves WHY. Why is this the relationship that I want to be in?" Grandma Gjertrud suddenly realized she was getting way off track, and immediately stopped talking. "Sorry honey, that was unnecessary. I will stick to your thoughts and feelings. I think that's a big enough challenge as it is."

Karoline paused for a moment and then began talking. "When I met Peter, I was so proud. He was the first boy I had ever dated and I let him kiss me on the first date. I was so sure he was the right guy for me. As the years went by we studied together and shared a flat with some friends. Being together was like a habit, part of my daily life. He was my closest friend. I don't think I ever asked myself what he was and what he might want, much less what I wanted for myself. As long as we weren't quarreling I was actually quite happy. If I look at it from the outside it seems to me like I was playing house with him. Still I am sure I would have said that I loved him. Guess I might still say the same today."

"So what was it that made this change, Karoline? Have you any idea what happened?"

"We bought the house," Karoline said. "I think that is when it started to feel more serious to me. We had been working for a while, and with two full wages we could manage to buy a house. That was a big day. I guess it took my 'playing house' dream a big leap forward, so I started to talk about us having our own child. To me that sounded like a perfectly natural next step to take after getting the house."

"How did Peter feel about having a child?" Grandma Gjertrud asked.

"He didn't want to talk about it. He gave me all these weird excuses like: "We have to talk about that later; I want my promotion first; we have to pay down our mortgage a bit more before we can do that; I would like us to travel before we become parents" and a lot of other strange things."

"When you think about it now, what did he really try to tell you by saying these things?"

"I don't know," Karoline said, although a thought was beginning to form in her head. "He didn't want to have children?"

"Sounds that way to me," Grandma Gjertrud replied. "For some reason he did not want the two of you to have children. Can you think of why that was so?"

"I can think of more than one reason," Karoline said.

"That's good. Since we don't know what his intentions were, all we can do is let you talk about it, to see if you are able to feel what is right and wrong in your thoughts about this situation."

"I think that when I started talking about us having a baby, he realized that he didn't want to be with me anymore. Actually when I say that out loud, it feels true to me," Karoline admitted.

"Sounds true to me, too," Grandma Gjertrud commented.

"He might, by then, have started to see my friend. No, that doesn't feel right," Karoline said. She was surprised that two similar statements could make her feel totally different inside.

"I think I agree with you on that as well," Grandma Gjertrud said.

"But as I continued to talk about wanting a child, he got more scared and started to talk to his friends about it. I guess that's how he ended up with Ilse. He went to talk with her about it all. That sounds right to me," Karoline said. Grandma Gjertrud nodded.

"He felt I didn't understand him. Right. He felt too ashamed to admit he didn't like me after all these years. True. He kept away from home a lot, hoping I would stop liking him. Could be true, could be false… Oh, my God," Karoline said. She was totally overwhelmed. "I can feel the difference between right and wrong in my body. Is that what you do too, Grandma Gjertrud?"

"More or less," Grandma Gjertrud replied. "When I listen inwards I use some more parts of me, but I think you are doing really well, Karoline. You should be proud of yourself."

"I am," Karoline admitted.

"In my experience, this way of looking at a familiar situation can work really well in many cases. Be on your guard, though. If you're scared – scared of being hurt, scared the other person is cheating on you or whatever – your mind can play tricks on you."

Karoline nodded.

"So what do you think of him now, Karoline, this man you lived with for ten years? What kind of man is he?"

"He is weak, but he is honest, and he doesn't want to hurt me," Karoline said without hesitation.

"I believe you're right, Karoline," Grandma Gjertrud said softly. "I can sense there are still a lot of feelings there, but you have done very well for now."

After dinner, their neighbor, Ingrid, came to invite them all to a Barn Dance that coming Friday.

"We are celebrating the safe harvest of the first hay," she said, "And there will be a lot of people there since so many youngsters are home for the summer holidays."

"That would be lovely, Ingrid. Thank you!" said Grandma. "And Karoline and I would like to invite you to our little *polterabend* tomorrow evening. Would you like to join us?"

"I'd love to!" answered Ingrid. "I can't remember the last time I was invited to a hen night. Perfect timing, I guess!" she smiled. "Would you like me to bring the other two girls as well?"

"Do that," Grandma Gjertrud said. "I would love to share this event with all our champagne-celebration girls. Let's say six o'clock, shall we?"

As Karoline was getting ready for bed that night, Grandma Gjertrud came to give her a present. It was a little book, covered in a beautiful colored satin, much like the one she had given her as a teenager.

"Asking for help is important whenever you want to grow. I know I have already given you many tools that you can use to help yourself, but with this book I would like to issue you a challenge. Write down three things every evening that you would like some help with. After doing this for a while, you will be surprised to see how much help and support you receive from all kinds of unexpected places."

"That sounds great!" Karoline replied happily. "Thank you! I'll let you know how I make out."

As she climbed into bed, she wondered what to write in her new journal, but then made up her mind. Her list looked like this:

Tomorrow I need help on how to:

1. *Start to develop the woman inside me so I can find a new partner.*

2. *Get something to wear for the Barn Dance – preferably a red dress.*

3. *Understand myself and what I want from life.*

Then she closed her book and hid it under her pillow before lying down to sleep.

Bedtime Story Number Eighteen

"I don't have anything to wear to the barn dance, Grandma Gjertrud," Karoline said as they were eating breakfast. "Do you think there might be some clothes here my size that I could borrow?"

"Perhaps," Grandma Gjertrud replied. "Come here and let me measure you."

Karoline found it a bit odd that Grandma Gjertrud had to measure her all over to be able to tell her size, but as Grandma Gjertrud was good at making and repairing clothes, she didn't think much about it.

"What do you think we should serve our guests at the *polterabend?*" Grandma Gjertrud asked.

"I have no idea," Karoline answered. She wasn't used to making such decisions. Peter had always been a splendid cook and he had always taken care of the food at parties. She thought for a minute. "How about smoked salmon, scrambled eggs, and a nice creamy nettle puree? We could serve it with new potatoes and flatbread."

"Sounds terrific! Thank you!" Grandma Gjertrud replied.

"Can I ask you to help me decorate the room too?"

"Sure," Karoline said. "Where are we going to hold the party?"

"In the old lecture room. The stone wall there will be perfect for smashing china. I'm really looking forward to this little gathering, Karoline, especially the china smashing part. I haven't done that since I was your age, or even younger."

"How would you like the room decorated?" Karoline asked.

"I was thinking of using a white tablecloth, nice flowers from the garden, crystal and porcelain serving dishes, and maybe some silverware. And some nicely folded napkins. I'll leave the details up to you. You have an eye for that kind of thing and I know you've always been good at the napkin stuff," Grandma Gjertrud grinned.

"I have Oscar on the phone here," Uncle Bernt shouted from the living room. "He would like to offer you a free Ma-uri massage session sometime tomorrow, Karoline. Would you like that?"

Karoline didn't know what to say. She had never heard of Ma-uri massage before and was somewhat skeptical of massage in general. Still, she had to admit it was a tempting offer. "Is he good?" she whispered to Grandma Gjertrud.

"Oh yes, he is good," Grandma Gjertrud answered. "Really good!"

"Okay, tell him I'd love to, thank you," Karoline shouted back to Uncle Bernt.

"Can I ask you something?" Karoline turned back to face Grandma.

"Any time, honey!"

"Why were you so angry with me yesterday?"

"I'm not sure I follow you," Grandma Gjertrud said sounding puzzled.

"When you cut me off yesterday, saying 'I'm not having this', or something like that," Karoline responded.

"Oh, now I understand," Grandma Gjertrud replied. "I was not angry with you, but I didn't want to play your game. Picking a fight to vent your frustrations is not my style and wouldn't have helped you a bit. I don't know if you do that with other people, but I won't let you do it with me. So I said no. Simple as that. I realize you're vulnerable at the moment, so I should have been a bit more diplomatic, but the conclusion is still the same. Why do you play this game, Karoline? Was Peter often angry?"

"No, I can't really say he was." Karoline replied. "I guess it's more the feeling of being conquered that I remember from the water experiments we used to do with Uncle Bernt. I felt overwhelmed by your straightforwardness. I will have to work on that again."

"Yes, you will. Can I add something, though?"

"Sure."

"It has to do with anger and how we usually view it. Do you remember what Mahatma Ghandi said? 'An eye for an eye makes the whole world blind.' "

"Yes, we learned about him in school."

"And what do you think he meant when he said that?"

"You tell me," Karoline said.

"Well, the thing is, in those days people would often perform justice according to their own private laws or family rules. You hit me – I hit you; you kill my son - I kill your son; you hurt my eye – I hurt your eye. In short, they would return violence with more violence which is often referred to as 'an eye for an eye.' Ghandi explained how that could never stop the anger process unless you altered the system of justice. In the meantime, he still wanted to work for non-violence, inspiring people to *be the change that you want to see in the world*' and stop the cycle of anger and violence."

"But why are you telling me this?" Karoline asked.

"This morning you were angry, and you wanted to throw that anger at me because it made you feel bad and you wanted to get rid of that feeling. You didn't know what else to do with it. Anger is a great feeling; we just need to learn new ways of expressing it. For instance, anger has a natural place in the grieving process. You experience a loss and that makes you feel numb, but later you feel your sadness really strongly, maybe so strongly that the only way for you to deal with it is to close off your heart. Then sooner or later you will find you feel angry. That is a big emotional shift because unlike the other feelings, anger fills you with energy. The big question is how do you want to use that energy? This morning your energy was starting to return, just enough to question some of my advice, trying to make me defend myself so you could criticize me some more, throwing this extra energy back at someone close. I'm guessing it was actually Peter you wanted to harm with it."

"I guess you're right," Karoline said. She was quite surprised at the way this conversation was developing, but at the same time she noticed that what she was feeling in her body told her this was *true* as opposed to *false*.

"My point is that you're not supposed to harm anyone with this anger energy. You're supposed to transform it, to use it as a way of lifting yourself, a way of transforming your situation making it possible for you to move on. Having access to power means making sure you use that power responsibly, for the best or with love, if you prefer those expressions. To sum up, I am glad to see that you are making your way through your grieving process in a very good way. I also wanted to point out to you that you can use this powerful anger that's coming through you in a more positive manner. Express this power through love and use it to lift yourself to the next stage of your life."

"Amen," Uncle Bernt said trying to hide his smile as he came into the room.

"Hallelujah!" Grandma Gjertrud responded and they both started laughing. "Thank you for helping me to get out of the mindfulness I sometimes dive into, sailor. Right, time for lunch. I'm starving! How about you two?"

"I am so hungry I can hardly move my feet," Karoline said in a theatrical voice that made Grandma Gjertrud laugh even harder.

As the guests arrived for the *polterabend* that evening, Karoline was surprised to find her old friend Anne among them.

"Anne, how good to see you!" Karoline said. "I didn't know you were one of Grandma Gjertrud's best friends!"

"Yes, I still help her with the painting groups, just like the ones she used to have," Anne said, hugging her old friend. "Actually, now I am the one in charge. Gjertrud prefers to sit with her sewing machine these days!

"Wow, that's great!" Karoline replied. She suddenly remembered the problems they'd had at the start of their high school years when it looked like they would never speak again. Then Anne had decided to join Grandma Gjertrud's painting class and here she was, still painting, while Karoline had hardly touched a brush since she met Peter. "I'm so glad that you and Grandma Gjertrud are helping each other. It must be great for her to have you as a business partner."

"Yes, I am very grateful to her, but most of all I am grateful to you, Karoline, for having invited me to join that first painting class. It has made all the difference in my life, that's for sure."

"I really want to start smashing all this beautiful china right away," Ingrid giggled as soon as they were all gathered in the lecture room, "But can we have some instructions please?" She eyed the bags of china that they'd all brought with them.

"Okay," replied Grandma Gjertrud. "I'll give you the short version. The *polterabend* is a German wedding tradition. The way I am used to doing it is a bit different to the old German way, but I like mine better."

"Why am I not surprised?" Ingrid said grinning broadly.

Grandma Gjertrud playfully stuck her tongue out at Ingrid and said, "If I might continue... We are doing this for several reasons: to have fun, to get rid of some old china in a great way, to break some old habits, and to release some emotions in the process. In connection with weddings, it is also about destroying the way back, making forward the only way to go as all the old things are broken and thrown away. We'll use this corner over here, where both the floor and the wall are made of stone. You can throw forwards or backwards, although I like the forward style. It gives me more control, which means I can throw harder. Who wants to start?"

"I do." Karoline was surprised to hear her own voice speak out. She grabbed one of the plates in front of her, walked over toward the wall, and raised her hand. She felt like a handball player as she threw the plate hard against the wall, watching it break in many pieces and fall down to the floor.

"Good shot," Grandma Gjertrud said. "Who's next?"

They all had a great time smashing china before Grandma Gjertrud finished it all off by taking a big stack of plates, holding them out in front of her, and just opening her hands, letting go of all the plates simultaneously. "Oops," she said. "Guess I just dropped some china!"

Everybody loved the food and afterwards as they were each enjoying a glass of wine, Ingrid suddenly said, "Why don't we come to the Barn Party without underwear tomorrow night? I have heard that's a cool thing to do."

"Where on earth have you heard that?" one of the other ladies said.

"Some friends of mine have told me they get so much attention when they go out without underwear. I have been meaning to try it myself sometime, but I always forget," Ingrid went on.

"But isn't that a bit vulgar?" Karoline couldn't imagine herself going out to the garden without underwear let alone going to a party.

"But honey, no one will know," Ingrid said grinning. "We won't tell anyone, and it won't be visible."

"But what's the point in doing it if nobody knows about it?" Karoline was really confused.

"*We* will know about it. That's the kick," said Ingrid. "And because we know, we will behave differently. My friends tell me that they find men treat them differently, showing them more respect and being far more attentive, when they go to parties without their underwear. I'm giving it a try, tomorrow night. Anyone else in?"

Nobody said a word, and then Grandma Gjertrud suddenly spoke. "Well, I've read glossy magazines at the dentist's office and from what I can tell, pop stars and actresses do this all the time. Why should they have all the fun? I'm in too, Ingrid!"

Karoline gasped in shock. Was this really her big, warm, cozy, wise grandmother speaking?

I'm never going to a party without my underwear, that's for sure, she thought.

Then someone else made a joke and they all laughed and told funny stories until late, all thriving in each other's company. As Karoline said goodbye to the last guest, she suddenly realized that this was the best party she had ever been to.

Bedtime Story Number Nineteen

Karoline came down later than usual the next morning. She found both Grandma Gjertrud and Uncle Bernt waiting for her in the kitchen, smiling like there was something special going on.

"We have a surprise for you today," they said together.

"Really?" Karoline grinned and hugged them good morning. "I love surprises! What is it?"

"We've decided to treat you to a day of pampering," Grandma Gjertrud said. "I guess it was Oscar who gave us the idea. We thought that since you are going to town for your Ma-uri massage, you might as well see the hairdresser, too. No offence, but your hair could do with some professional care. When we spoke to the hairdresser, she told us the manicurist and pedicurist both had some time free, so we booked you in for appointments with them, too. I hope you don't mind us planning all this for you, honey!"

"Of course not! This is wonderful! I have never had a manicure or a pedicure. Thank you both very, very much!"

"I will be your driver today," Uncle Bernt said. "Your Grandma is busy with some preparations for tonight. I suggest we treat ourselves to lunch in a lovely little restaurant I know of as well. The car will be ready at ten thirty. Will that suit you, my lady?" Uncle Bernt bowed in front of Karoline, who giggled and grinned at Grandma. "Very well, then," he said, and left the room.

"Did you manage to find any clothes to fit me?" Karoline asked Grandma Gjertrud.

"I haven't had a chance to look yet, but I'm pretty sure I have something approximately your size," she replied casually.

"That's great. I would hate to have to buy something new right now, when I don't know what is going to happen with my finances and everything."

"Don't worry," Grandma Gjertrud said, with a mysterious little smile on her face.

"Grandma Gjertrud," Karoline said. "Why did you decide to join the no-underwear group tonight? It's not really what I would have expected of you."

Grandma Gjertrud started laughing. "Meaning that seeing as I'm so old, or me being big, or me being what, Karoline?" Grandma Gjertrud replied, still laughing.

"I don't know," Karoline said. She was confused. "I thought it was a good thing to be a respectable person, and I would never expect a respectable person to go to a party without wearing underwear. So what in the world has happened here? That's what I don't get."

"Honey," Grandma Gjertrud said. "You have been living together with a man for almost ten years. You must have had sex, enjoying yourself and everything. I, on the contrary, have lived alone for ages, so now that I finally have a man in my house, I can tell you there is no way I am going to play by any respectable rules if they don't fit my needs. To me sex is about pleasure and having fun together. It's about being curious, open for new ways of doing things, or saying no to other things if you feel like doing that. To sum up, it is about *joy*, and I want more joy in my life. So when someone tells me this is a fun thing to do, and I can easily tell that it must be safe to do, I think, what the heck – I'm in!"

Karoline's jaw dropped and she looked at Grandma Gjertrud. She was just about to say something when Uncle Bernt shouted that it was time to leave.

253

"Thank you, Grandma Gjertrud," she said and walked over to give her a big hug. "Thank you for being honest with me. I can see I have a lot to learn."

"You already know the most important stuff, honey. The rest will follow, as long as you are open to hearing about life. Always remember to live your life by your own standards, and don't get confused if my standards are not the same as yours. We will always love each other, anyhow. Always, honey!"

The first stop on Karoline's Pampering List was to see Oscar and have one of his Ma-uri massages. Karoline had never heard about this type of massage before, but was looking forward to having her body soothed after days of having a tight chest and experiencing shallow breathing due to her anger. Oscar looked like a nice man. He was a friend of Uncle Bernt's, although obviously a lot younger. His massage room was very plain, containing only a massage table, a stereo rack with lots of CD's, a shelf with some nice pieces of art, and a burning candle. Underneath the massage table was a little bowl of water heated from underneath by a candle. In the bowl of water a bottle of massage oil was warming.

"If you would remove all your clothes then lie face down on the bench, I will be with you in a couple of minutes," he said.

Karoline froze. "Did he say *all* of my clothes?" she wondered. Karoline was about to walk out the door when she remembered the conversation with Grandma Gjertrud and could still hear her words inside her head. "It is about *joy*" and "If others tell me it is fun, and I can see that it is safe… "

Karoline suddenly felt inside that this was a safe thing to do. She quickly took her clothes off and lay down on the table. The room smelled of something nice, but she couldn't tell what it was.

Then Oscar entered the room. He was wearing a piece of cloth around his waist, covering his body down to his ankles. He put a big towel on top of her and started off holding his hands on her back as if to listen to her body. He then put some soothing music on, pulled the towel downwards uncovering the upper half of her body, and poured some warm oil onto her skin. The massage itself was very special and definitely felt good. Oscar used all of his body to make the movements, long dynamic pulls and gentle swings, all following the music.

Karoline soon noticed how all her body was just letting go into this dynamic movement happening between two people and carefully chosen music. She could feel her mind wandering off on its own as she stopped thinking and just let go. Half way into the session Oscar asked her to turn around. She did so without hesitating, letting go of all feelings of being naked alone with a man, as he carefully moved the towel all the time covering some of her body while working somewhere else.

When the massage ended, Oscar wrapped her in towels and blankets, telling her to relax and let the treatment settle in her body before getting up to leave.

"You look ten years younger, sweetie," Uncle Bernt commented when he picked her up after the massage. "Now we are going to get some lunch," he said, opening the door of the massage salon for her on their way out. "After you, Miss."

Karoline noticed that something inside her was starting to wake up and stretch when Uncle Bernt treated her like this and it felt new to her. It was as if she had never been seen by a man before although she had lived with one for more than ten years. *How strange*, she said to herself. *This is so new to me.* But she was not able to tell what this thing awakening in her actually was.

The hairdresser and manicurist took good care of her, making her feel so special that she was glowing by the end of the appointment. The hairdresser even offered to give her some free make-up as an extra service.

"My goodness, is this beauty still you?" Uncle Bernt said when she came out of the wellness center." You look like a real princess and that sure suits you, sweetie! Now I am going to escort you to the shoe shop to get you some suitable dancing shoes for tonight. This is my special treat for you. I have always loved a woman to wear good looking shoes. What would you like? High-heel sandals, to show off your painted toenails?"

Karoline was speechless, but she was still so relaxed from all her pampering that she allowed herself to be led into the shoe shop and shown some beautiful high-heeled sandals with little diamonds all over them. She was surprised at how easily she could move in them.

"That is because they are high quality shoes, my dear," the owner of the shop told her. "Always go for good quality; it is so much better for your feet."

"My lady will take these sandals," Uncle Bernt said. He had noticed that Karoline loved the shoes, but had also discovered they were running late for the Barn Party.

Back at the farm, Grandma Gjertrud was delighted to see the change in Karoline, not just in her physical appearance, but in her vibration, too. "You look gorgeous, honey!" she cried. "I have always said that women recover and get their power from pleasure, but I don't think I have ever seen it as clearly as today." Grandma pointed at Karoline's new shoes. "He has done a great job, that sailor of mine! Now, I have an extra surprise for you, too. I'll just go and get it."

Karoline heard Grandma Gjertrud go upstairs into Karoline's old bedroom. There were some rustles and a thump, and then she appeared back downstairs carrying a red dress. "This should fit you perfectly," she smiled, "Unless my math is totally wrong."

When Karoline realized that Grandma Gjertrud had made her this dress today, she started crying. "Oh no," Grandma Gjertrud said, crestfallen. "Don't tell me I picked the wrong color. Bernt insisted you wanted a red dress, but I thought you might have looked good in turquoise. I should have remembered he is predisposed to red dresses and not to be relied upon in such matters. I'm sorry, honey. Would you consider wearing it anyway?"

Karoline wiped her eyes with the back of her hand, sniffed and laughed. She started to explain that this was the exact color she had dreamed of having, that Bernt was not mistaken, and that her tears were those of joy and gratitude. Grandma looked relieved.

"Please try it on!" she said. "It's always so exciting to see ladies try their new clothes on for the first time!"

Karoline went up to her room. She removed all her old clothes, put on a new bra, and let the dress fall over her body head to toe. She immediately knew that this was The Dress. She had never felt as beautiful and chic before. As she came dancing down into the kitchen she could hear Uncle Bernt's recognition and Grandma Gjertrud's sigh.

"You look gorgeous, honey!" she said.

"We'd better get ourselves ready too, love," Uncle Bernt said to Grandma Gjertrud. "Karoline, get yourself something to eat. You will be dancing all evening so make sure you have enough energy to cope!" he shouted to her from the bathroom.

The barn was beautifully decorated with green, leafy branches and summer flowers. The music was already playing as the three of them entered. Karoline could see some familiar faces, but there were also many unknown to her. Tonight this did not make her feel uncomfortable at all. She felt on top of the world. Many of the men immediately noticed the gorgeous woman in red, and soon she was approached by one of them asking her for a dance.

Karoline was surprised at how quickly she got used to being surrounded by men treating her with admiration and respect. Even the old farmers who came to talk to her when they were drunk enough to dare did not bother her, as she found she could easily talk to them in a polite and friendly way, but still keep the situation under control. When Uncle Bernt came to say it was time to go home, she was surprised to find they had been at the party for more than six hours.

"This has been the best day of my life," Karoline said as they walked into the kitchen after arriving home from the dance. "Thank you so much, both of you, for making this thing happen to me!" she said.

"Thank *you*, Karoline, for being such a fantastic girl, lighting up our whole community this evening. It was a thrill to watch you enjoy yourself on the dance floor and I must admit I was proud to know you," Grandma Gjertrud replied.

"Give my compliments to your tailor, as that dress was the best I have ever seen," Uncle Bernt grinned, and laughing, they all headed off to bed.

Bedtime Story Number Twenty

Karoline woke up feeling different the next morning. It was like her whole body had been through a total makeover. She slowly recaptured the feeling of having her nails done on both her hands and feet, her hair cut in a chic way, and wearing beautiful high-heeled sandals with diamonds. She remembered the joy of eating lunch with Uncle Bernt, and being massaged… naked!

No, I didn't! she told herself, like it was something to be ashamed of. *Yes, I did, and I loved it!* Karoline froze. *Who said that?* she thought. Suddenly she understood that this voice was also hers, but it was as if this was another part of her speaking, a part that she had never known was there. Then she remembered getting a new dress, a red dress. She recaptured the feeling of it moving gracefully around her body. And she had been dancing – a lot.

Laughing. Smiling. Telling jokes. Being surrounded by nice men. And women. And wearing … no underwear. *No, I didn't!* she tried telling herself. *Yes, I did, and I'm definitely going to do it again!* The voice, which was not really a voice, more like a knowing, was getting more intense.

I get it, she thought. *I'm dreaming!* She laughed as she realized this was definitely too good to be true. *Me... surrounded by nice men, all asking me to dance? Nice try, Karoline. We can do that dream again. Any time!* The thought made her relax, although it also made her a bit sad. She would have loved for it to be true, all of it.

That's when she turned around in her bed and found herself looking straight at a beautiful red dress draped over a chair. On the floor beside it stood a pair of high-heeled sandals set with diamonds.

She jumped up and ran down to the kitchen wearing only her nightgown.

"Good morning, sweetie!" Uncle Bernt greeted her from his place at the table. "Seen a ghost or something?"

"Tell me I'm not dreaming!" she cried.

"Dreaming? Dreaming what? Nothing close to what all the guys surrounding you last night might have been dreaming, I'm sure," he laughed. "No, sweetie, I can assure you, you were the queen of the Barn Dance last night, and you've got yourself a lot of guys still dreaming of you. Good on you!"

"Did you have a good sleep?" Grandma Gjertrud asked. She looked concerned. It had been a big day yesterday for Karoline and she wondered how she was coping with it all.

"Yes, I slept peacefully all night," she said as she sat down to join them at the breakfast table. "It was just this morning as I started to remember some things about yesterday that I thought I must have been dreaming. But I wasn't! What a pleasant surprise!"

"I'll make you some bacon and eggs," Uncle Bernt suggested. "You must be starving having spent half the night dancing."

"Oh, I'd love that, thank you. Can I ask you to make me some fried tomatoes with basil as well?"

"Coming right up, sweetie!"

"I'm going home tomorrow," Karoline said suddenly. "I need to start packing up my part of the things in the house and arrange for some friends to come over to help me move all the stuff. I don't know where to move yet, but I guess that's just a minor detail!" Karoline was surprised she could joke about having nowhere to live, but as she did, she felt really nice and warm inside.

"I have always pictured you moving here when your parents decide to hand over the farm," Grandma Gjertrud mumbled, but no one seemed to notice.

"Let me know if you need help moving your stuff," Uncle Bernt interrupted. "I could always take the van. Gjertrud and I would be happy to help if there is anything we can do, wouldn't we, darling?"

"Certainly. I'd love to come over and have a look at your new place, Karoline. Just give us a call and a day's notice. Good old work horses like Bernt and me might still have something to contribute."

Uncle Bernt got up from the table. "I'm going out to get on with some work," he said. "I'll leave you girls to do some talking."

"Can we make some tea and talk about some woman stuff?" Karoline asked as he went out of the door.

"Oh, yes. Perfect timing," Grandma Gjertrud replied.

"This morning I had this new voice or feeling, or kind of knowing, that I haven't had before," Karoline began. "Can you help me understand what that is?"

"I need you to tell me more about that, Karoline."

"As I remembered the Ma-uri massage, something in me tried to deny it had ever happened, but at the same time something else in me told me very clearly that it did happen, and that I did enjoy it. I have never had this feeling of duality before. How can that be?"

"Which of these two statements are yours, Karoline?" Grandma Gjertrud asked.

"I believe they both are and that's what puzzles me."

"I believe you're right, Karoline. But why would a part of you try to deny the fact that you had Ma-uri massage yesterday?"

"Because it was scared maybe?"

"It was scared? Of what?"

"Of being hurt maybe?"

"In what way hurt, do you think?"

"Being unable to protect myself."

"But why did you feel you needed to protect yourself? What was there to hurt you?"

"I was naked in a room with a half-naked man. I guess that triggered some things in me."

"Are you trying to say that you were afraid you would be raped?"

Karoline had to think that one over for a minute.

"No. To be honest I was not afraid of that. I don't feel that sex really has anything to do with this."

"I agree. So I am asking you again. What was there to be afraid of in that situation? You were totally protected. Both Uncle Bernt and I are perfectly capable of discovering people's hidden, bad intentions, and had guaranteed to you this was a safe thing to do. So what made you feel unsafe?"

"I think that I feel unsafe most of the time. It's probably for no real reason, but I still feel that way. So what can I do about it?"

"Now I believe we are seeing the essence of your question. Meaning we can start to look for the answer.

Would you like my opinion on this?" Grandma Gjertrud asked.

"Desperately!"

"Okay. Now, let's see if I can make this simple," Grandma Gjertrud began. "The way I perceive this is that you have been extremely open during your life, meaning easy to overwhelm; meaning your waves were very soft if we are to talk about the stones-in-the-water analogy. Not necessarily weak, not even few, but soft. And what would be your best shot for curing that, Karoline?"

"Increasing my inner vibrancy?"

"I'm proud of you, honey. You're beginning to understand. Okay, so here we have this girl with soft vibrations who has a hard time protecting herself against other people's influences. She's learned some ways of keeping her vibrations high and strong, but she doesn't practice them, mostly because she doesn't realize how important it is to do so. Now, this girl falls in love with a guy; plays 'house' with him for a while. She never asks herself what she wants because his waves are interfering with hers all the time, making it hard for her to listen to herself. She's not aware that she is playing by his rules, and besides, to her they all seem like her rules anyway. He is not violent, he is not trying to dominate her, he is just being himself. She loves him and lets him enter her heart because she's been taught that that is what you do when you're in love. Now he is even touching her heart with his vibrations, but somehow there's always something missing. No matter what he does, he can never find her essence. The problem is that he passed her essence long ago without even noticing. Does this make sense to you, Karoline?"

"Yes!"

"If you think of the stones-in-the-water analogy, can you use that to tell me exactly at what point he passed her essence without realizing it?"

Karoline had to think hard on this one, but then came up with an answer she felt had to be right. "As the waves from the two stones met! As they touched each other for the first time, before his waves overrode hers!"

"Exactly!" Grandma Gjertrud said. "Your essence, your vibration, your radiation, your energy, your YOU – call it whatever you want, collided with his.

The point is he never noticed it. He never saw it. So there he is, stumbling around in your heart, looking for your essence, thinking you are hiding it from him and keeping him at a distance for some reason. The thought occurs to him that you must be less devoted to this relationship than he is. This scares him and hurts him so much, he starts pulling away, and then he dumps you. You are taken by surprise because you thought you were giving him everything. You feel shocked and think that you are never going to survive this. To protect yourself, you chose to shut down the place where you hurt the most. What place would that be, Karoline?"

Karoline started crying. "My heart," she said.

Even Grandma Gjertrud cried. They both sat there crying, saying nothing for quite a while.

"That is what you tried to tell me when I came the other day," Karoline said softly.

"It was, honey," Grandma Gjertrud replied. "I saw that you had closed your heart, but I could not understand why, because I could not reach through your protection to see the reason. Normally when people say someone has broken their heart, they don't have to shut it off because they can just repair it again, but yours looked totally shut down.

"Now I realize I could have taught you even more while you were still young, helped you develop your essence so that it would have been safe for you to keep your heart open all the time, making it easier for you to survive in a relationship. How can I ever forgive myself," Grandma Gjertrud said. She obviously blamed herself for this neglect.

"But I am still here," Karoline reminded her. "I even think that I am starting to mend. I think that what you told me during those first days here was true. As I started my work to increase my inner vibration, I got stronger. My essence got stronger. That meant I could start trying new things, and with the help of you and Uncle Bernt, a day full of pampering, a fantastic red dress, some gorgeous high-heeled sandals, and a Barn Dance, I discovered that my vibration became massively increased and my essence was out there starting to radiate. This made me feel more protected, and in turn made me lose the need to shut down my heart, since nobody was going to be able to get to my heart without first having to pass my vibrations, which will not be so easy to overwhelm anymore.

"So what you are now telling me, Karoline, is that the voice you talked about this morning, the one being afraid and thinking you might be attacked or hurt, that voice is about to shut up?"

"Yes," Karoline said. "I think that that is what I experienced this morning. I think that this other voice, this new voice of mine starting to grow in me, is the voice of my heart wanting to mend, of me wanting to live fully, showing off my essence to the world, contributing with all my wisdom, my knowledge, my intuition, and my love."

"Thank you, Karoline!" Grandma Gjertrud said. "Thank you for helping me mend my former mistakes. You sure are a soft, but oh so wise young woman. I am really proud of you, honey!"

Bedtime Story Number Twenty-One

"I would like to go to church today," Grandma Gjertrud said next morning. "Would you like to accompany me, Karoline?"

"Yes! I haven't been in a church for ages, so I guess that would be nice. Isn't Uncle Bernt coming?"

"No, he's not much for visiting churches, I'm afraid," Grandma Gjertrud said, without even a hint of blaming him for that. "Bernt tends to find his God in nature. He will probably take a walk in the woods to have some solitude this morning. He is a good man, my Bernt. He takes time to refresh himself. He even takes pride in dealing with his emotional baggage without involving me."

"Why would you be involved in him getting rid of his baggage?" Karoline asked. She was surprised.

"Because of their close connection to Mother Nature, women have a natural talent for helping others get their vibrations back in alignment if they've gotten out of alignment somehow. This can be done on an unconscious level. Highly spiritual women have a greater ability for doing this, often unconsciously helping people realign their vibrations, but it will be even more successful if done on a conscious level."

"I am not sure I follow you," Karoline said. "Can you try to explain it in an easier way?"

"Well, look at it like this," said Grandma Gjertrud. "Think about Mother Nature and all she's capable of doing. No matter how polluted and out of balance things get, she's always able to restore order and harmony. Her great cycles break down even the most toxic substances and recycle them in ways that benefit us all. Mother Nature's great cycles provide us with fresh, clean air to breathe, fresh, clean water, and nourishing food to eat. And all this is constantly happening without us even realizing it. Are you with me so far, Karoline?"

"I am. It's amazing when you think about it!" Karoline said.

"It sure is and still we tend to take it for granted! Anyway, I was trying to explain to you that a woman, because of her nature, the way she is put together, the things that make her a woman in the first place, because of all this she is capable of doing a lot of things that will support both a *man* and *mankind*. She can, for instance, help others by healing things that trouble them on a vibrational level. She will often do this for the men in her surroundings without either of them realizing what she is doing."

"But if this is going on without them realizing, why is it a problem?" Karoline wanted to know.

"That is an important question, Karoline!" Grandma Gjertrud said. She was grateful for the fact that Karoline seemed to be following her explanation. For awhile now she'd had a sense that she might not be part of this earthly life much longer, and she desperately hoped that Karoline would be the one to whom she could pass down her knowledge.

"So we said that Mother Nature is good at recycling toxic matter and transforming it into harmless, even helpful things. She seems to do this effortlessly, at no cost to herself, yet experts are now warning us that even our Great Mother is starting to struggle under the strain of too many toxins. Balance is being lost and the delicate web of life is starting to break down. This applies to women, too. Womankind on Earth is starving. They are suffering because men do not understand, much less take part in, keeping harmony among people. As women we will go on doing our part continuously without even realizing it, because that's just how we're made. This means that the more emotional baggage a man carries home, the more his partner will clear it for him. The problem is that because this usually happens unconsciously, many women will experience the same thing you recently went through. They will get hurt, their hearts will block, and they will find themselves in a downward spiral that sucks away their desire for life and leaves them wide open to whatever disease can kill them." Grandma Gjertrud stopped talking and looked at Karoline.

"Wow!" Karoline said. She had tears running down her face, and quickly realized Grandma Gjertrud had, too. "Wow!" she said one more time. "I am glad I know you, Grandma Gjertrud! I could have died, couldn't I?"

"Yes, you could have, honey," Grandma nodded. "You could have died."

"But why do we not get told this stuff? Why don't more people know about it?" Karoline wondered.

"I am telling *you*, Karoline. *You* will know. And *you* know how to turn this whole thing around, too, because you've just done it yourself." Grandma Gjertrud put a finger to her lips. Outside they could hear the familiar sound of the church bells drifting over the woods and fields from the village calling them all to come to service. "It's time to go to church," she said.

As the service ended, Grandma Gjertrud turned to Karoline and whispered, "Hurry up. There's something I want to show you. I've arranged for you to see inside the bell tower, but we need to get up there before John starts ringing the bell or we'll get him out of balance."

Karoline quickly followed Grandma through a little door she hadn't noticed before and found herself on a narrow staircase reaching all the way up the bell tower. They climbed and climbed, the stairs getting narrower and narrower, until at last they found themselves on a little wooden ladder at the very top. "Almost there, John!" Grandma cried breathlessly. She stopped for a second and breathed deeply, hands on her hips. Karoline climbed the ladder into the bell loft and Grandma followed slowly a moment later.

"I had no idea there was actually someone up here doing this job," Karoline said, shaking hands with the bell-ringer.

"Yes, some churches still ring their bells manually," John replied. "It's a tough job, physically, but you get into a magical rhythm as you go along. Put on some earmuffs," he added, pointing to a basket in the corner. "The point of bells is to be heard far away, not to care about the hearing of us being up here, I'm afraid."

John took a rope in each hand and started to pull the largest bell. Slowly, slowly, it started to turn. Just before the huge clapper inside hit the wall of the bell, he started pulling the second bell. It was entrancing to watch. At first there was no sound, only motion. Then as the clapper fell against the metal, a huge vibration burst out over the surrounding countryside. It was a sound felt as much as heard, reverberating deep inside their bodies and seeming to fill the whole world. Then the second bell sounded a higher note than the first and another huge pulse of energy rippled out across the land. Karoline was amazed as she realized that John had to pull each rope at a different pace in order to keep the sounding of the bells rhythmical and steady. It was fascinating to see him standing there between the bells, his two arms looking like they were living separate lives and yet the whole forming such an image of harmony and perfection.

Karoline grinned in delight and turned to share her joy with Grandma Gjertrud. As she did so, a sudden chill washed over her and the sound of the bells died away in her ears. She watched in horror as all the color drained from Grandma Gjertrud's face, replaced with a look of surprise. The old lady clutched at her chest, looked straight at Karoline, then stumbled backwards and disappeared over the edge of the platform.

Karoline's world froze. She could hear her heart thumping oh so slowly in her ears, and saw her own feet start to move towards the ladder. She saw John drop the bell ropes and noticed with fascination how the huge bells gradually came to a halt and all their vibrations died away into the morning sky.

Even before she reached the bottom of the ladder, Karoline knew that Grandma Gjertrud was dead. There she lay in the dust of the bell tower, her best Sunday clothes in disarray, a little smile on her face. Her handbag was still clutched to her, although it had fallen open. As she came closer, Karoline noticed that a little bell, an exact copy of the large church bell, had rolled out and was lying close by. Karoline reached out her hand, picked up the bell, and held it close to her heart while hot tears streamed down her face.

Karoline's Final Session with Grandma Gjertrud

Karoline's Life at Thirty-Six

K aroline sat in bed looking at the little church bell in her hands, waiting for Grandma Gjertrud to arrive. These last weeks had been full of surprises. Things were suddenly going much better in her life. Her boss and colleagues were now treating her with respect, her boyfriend was being more communicative and attentive, and her mood and energy had both improved as her nightly requests for help had been responded to in mysterious ways.

She ran her fingers over the cool, smooth metal, admiring the gentle glow of the bell in the lamp light.

As the bell started to jingle, a recognizing smile formed on her lips and she looked up. "Hello, Grandma Gjertrud," she said.

"Hello, honey. I see you still have the bell. I'm so glad you do. It was meant to be a gift for you, you see. After I'd shown you the big church bells, I was going to give you this and explain how bells work."

"How about you tell me now," Karoline said, smiling.

"Well," Grandma Gjertrud began, "All things – plants, animals, rocks, objects, emotions, have their own vibration, right? Only some things vibrate at a slower rate than others. Some things vibrate so slowly that the vibrations don't go very far at all, and the whole feeling around them becomes stagnant, dense, and heavy. This can happen in a house when people are feeling very sad or depressed, for example. They're vibrating so slowly that the vibrations can't go very far and they all build up around the edges of the rooms, making the space feel sad, like the people. When you ring a bell, it produces strong vibrations in the air, vibrations that you hear as sound. These sound vibrations have the ability to shatter the old, stuck, slow vibrations and clean them right out of the house. We say that ringing a bell can literally clean a space. Of course, you still have to get the hot soapy water out and clean the physical grime that collects around these low vibrations!" Grandma Gjertrud laughed. "Such sounds can also affect our body and mind," she continued, "Which is why they are popular in certain meditation techniques. But church bells can also do something else. They send out a calling – a calling for people to come forward, to take action. This is what I wanted to share with you that day in the bell tower with John. He wasn't just making a noise. He was calling all the people in, cleansing their auras, increasing their vibrations, and then sending them safely home again."

"I am sorry that I didn't understand much of what you were trying to tell me back in those days. I did see John pulling his ropes, but I didn't see him the way you help me see him now," Karoline said sadly.

"But remember," said Grandma Gjertrud, "I didn't know most of this stuff then either! It's only since I've been on the other side that so much has become clear to me. That's why this opportunity to teach you what I've learned is so precious. And you know, I wonder if we need to fail sometimes just to understand the importance of taking responsibility for ourselves."

"You mean the fact that I've been feeling like such a failure recently might help me understand how important it is to take proper care of myself?"

"Is that what's happened?"

"I must admit it is, Grandma Gjertrud. Having you visit me regularly these last weeks has been such a comfort, and I've loved hearing your stories and trying out your many exercises. I have actually come to call them *Peace Exercises*, as I feel the core of your teachings have been how women can help care for peace in the world. I've learned so much."

"By the way!" Karoline said, suddenly looking up at Grandma. "You remember the night you told me the bedtime story with me partying in that red dress, without my underwear? Well, the next day I decided to give it a go, and that evening, guess what? Hans called me, and told me he missed me! Hans... calling me on his travels? That was a first! He is normally so preoccupied in his work he totally forgets me when I am not there. Usually I am the one calling him to keep up our communication while he is away. So I guess there is really something to all the stuff about pleasure and letting people see your whole self, like I certainly did in that story of yours."

"Yes, Karoline. If I could only give you one piece of advice, it would be to take more time to seek pleasure, because in doing so we allow our true essence to unfold and we become the powerful, magical women we were born to be."

"I think what has surprised me the most, and even scared me a bit, is the realization that I already had most of the knowledge I needed inside me, but just never used it, " said Karoline.

"Yes, there's no point in dying of thirst because you won't drink the water in front of you," replied Grandma. "Through these bedtime stories I have covered the main reasons why you didn't take care of yourself, and I hope I've shown you that even the most caring, well-meaning parents can miss vital steps in their children's lives. But I have also tried to inspire you by giving you some new ways of solving your problems. Have you decided yet what action to take?"

Karoline nodded. "I have decided to work on increasing my vibration so I'll be able to hear my inner voice again. By doing that I hope to be able to open my heart and start healing it, so that eventually it will be safe to open myself up to a man, be it Hans or someone else. I realize now that although Hans has said he might leave me, I don't need to defend myself by rejecting him, pulling away, or getting scared. I can stay in my thought of wanting to give our relationship a chance and work from there. By staying in my own vibration, I can trust my inner voice to tell me along the way what will be best for me."

"Very good, Karoline. So your relationship is covered. Now what about your health? You were worried about your health?" Karoline noticed that Grandma Gjertrud's voice was beginning to sound weaker now.

"When you explained to me the other day how easily I could close my vibration down and open myself to disease, I just knew that it applied to me. I think that whatever's wrong with me will be mendable, as long as I work on strengthening my vibrations, opening my heart, and, of course, having lots of pleasure and fun! I don't think everyone is so lucky. I'm so glad the doctor caught whatever it is so early and that I have a chance to fix it."

Then they both sat there in complete silence, letting all the good things sink in. It was as if time stood still and they were almost scared to break the intense feeling of universal connection they were experiencing.

Karoline was the first to break the silence. "I need to ask you something."

"Certainly," replied Grandma.

"In the last bedtime story you mentioned that you had always pictured me taking over the farm. Strangely enough the idea has never struck me before, but now that I have come to think about it, I can feel some sort of longing to move back to the farm. Perhaps to use it as an oasis to give myself a closer connection to Mother Earth, and also a grounded place to work from. But do you think that I could manage to do that, Grandma Gjertrud?"

"Of course you can! Caring for Mother Nature is such an important job in this day and age, and at the same time a job that gives you so much in return. I am sure that you would be a brilliant small-scale farmer. You have both the practical knowledge from your childhood and the vibrational connection through your inner work. And then you can, of course, always ask me for advice, honey! I would love to see you being the next woman on 'my' farm. And if it is of any help to you, I know for a fact that your older brother Olaf has turned down the offer from your parents, so anyway you are the next in line of *odel,* your inherited birthright to the farm. Go for it, my girl, just do it!"

"Thank you for supporting me in this matter, Grandma. It means a lot to me to have your backing on making my final decision in this matter."

"But Grandma Gjertrud!" Karoline suddenly remembered. "You were in love with Uncle Bernt all those years weren't you?"

"Yes, I was," Grandma Gjertrud admitted. "Did you like my twist of letting him move in with me in these last bedtime stories?"

"Of course I did! It seemed like the most natural thing in the world. In the stories the two of you were so happy together! But why did you not let him move in with you while you were still alive, Grandma Gjertrud?"

"Oh," Grandma Gjertrud sighed. "Lots of reasons. I was scared, I had been hurt by men before, I was afraid he would turn me down, I thought I was too old to start a new relationship. I was scared he might think that I was too weird, too gross, too secretive, too opinionated, too demanding, and too masculine. I was worried that my old body would not be attractive to him. I could give you thousands of bad excuses, Karoline, with the last one being that I was a product of my time and upbringing and found it sinful in some way to live with a man without being married. The reason I'm showing you this is I want you to realize that all people, Indigo or not, can sometimes find it hard to believe in themselves. That is why communicating, sharing, and lifting each other's mood is always so important."

"Thank you so much for sharing all this with me Grandma Gjertrud," Karoline said. She could feel tears pushing behind her eyes and found it hard to speak. "And thank you for giving me such a great childhood, both in my real life and by retelling it through these stories. Loosing you so suddenly at such a young age was tough, but reconnecting with you through these past few weeks has helped me start to heal those scars in a nice way."

"It has been a pleasure, my darling Karoline," Grandma Gjertrud said softly. Her voice was so weak by now Karoline was scared she might disappear without saying goodbye.

"Can I ask you one more favor before you leave, Grandma Gjertrud?" Karoline said.

"Yes, honey."

"If I ever need you again, am I allowed to call upon you?"

"Any... time... ho... ne... y..." Grandma Gjertrud's voice faded away into the dark as did her soft appearance.

Karoline sat alone in the stillness and silence of her bedroom and looked around her. Then her eyes fell on the little bell now lying on her bedcovers. She picked it up, smiling, and shook it firmly, bringing out its loud and clear jingle, calling all her new dreams to her.

Printed in Great Britain
by Amazon